MW01088473

History of American Education
PRIMER

PETER LANG
New York • Washington, D.C./Baltimore • Bern
Frankfurt am Main • Berlin • Brussels • Vienna • Oxford

David Boers

History of American Education
PRIMER

PETER LANG
New York • Washington, D.C./Baltimore • Bern
Frankfurt am Main • Berlin • Brussels • Vienna • Oxford

Library of Congress Cataloging-in-Publication Data

Boers, David.
History of American education / David Boers.
p. cm.
Includes bibliographical references.
1. Education—United States—History. I. Title.
LA205.B68   370.973'09—dc22   2007006894
ISBN 978-1-4331-0036-9

Bibliographic information published by **Die Deutsche Bibliothek**.
Die Deutsche Bibliothek lists this publication in the "Deutsche
Nationalbibliografie"; detailed bibliographic data is available
on the Internet at http://dnb.ddb.de/.

Cover design by Clear Point Designs

The paper in this book meets the guidelines for permanence and durability
of the Committee on Production Guidelines for Book Longevity
of the Council of Library Resources.

© 2007 Peter Lang Publishing, Inc., New York
29 Broadway, 18th floor, New York, NY 10006
www.peterlang.com

All rights reserved.
Reprint or reproduction, even partially, in all forms such as microfilm,
xerography, microfiche, microcard, and offset strictly prohibited.

Printed in the United States of America

Contents

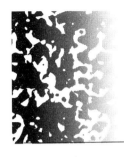

Ideological Management

As the Vehicle for the Evolution of American Education

Evolution of American education

The connected development of the American educational system from the 1630s to the present

Religious persecution

Depriving individuals and groups of their right to practice the religion of their choice

Basic principles

The expectation of citizens in the New England colonies to be God-fearing, father-obeying, and law-abiding

The **evolution of American education** has occurred since our nation was founded in the 1600s. Jonathan Winthrop and his band of followers sought to avoid **religious persecution** in England. They sailed to America and began to set up communities in the New England area that were meant to be models for what would eventually become American society. These early settlers sought to create a God-fearing, law-abiding society that would operate smoothly and be a stable force in people's lives, reflecting the principles of Puritan theology. Church leaders created societal rules and imparted the penalties for breaking them. Within these model communities began early forms of education, first informal and later formal. As logic would have it, the early leaders governed what was taught in schools.

Many factors came into play as education unfolded in America throughout the centuries. People took stands about which philosophies should represent the **basic principles** that would govern indi-

Good society

The society expected to be the result from living according to the basic principles

---

Divine intervention

The belief that God directs human lives

Primary factors

The philosophical, religious, social, economic, and political factors that have influenced the evolution of American education

---

Ideological managers

The individuals and groups who have controlled the ideas that have impacted the evolution of American education

viduals and schools and create the **good society**. Fervor for religion and strong belief in **divine intervention** caused people to pay strict attention to living according to God's will. Then, as time went on, religious differences raised the question of how to define society and its individuals. The question asked what types of individuals were desired to create what type of society. People discussed how individuals interact collectively for the common good and to form a good society. Much of this discussion developed through religious factors. The first economic considerations focused on getting the most out of living off the land. Eventually, however, economies became much more complex. Life became ever more expensive, and people expanded their economic desires. Politically, in the beginning, there was not much argument as to who the early political leaders were. No one argued much that Jonathan Winthrop and people like Noah Webster, Thomas Jefferson, Ben Franklin, and other early leaders received a great deal of respect for their ideas. In time, more people became politically involved in the building of our society, our schools, and our nation. Five elements stand out as clearly influencing education—philosophy, religion, social aspects, economics, and politics. The evolution of American education can be viewed through the development of these **primary factors** that shape its development. As these primary factors identified the focus at any time or during any period, they were accompanied by individuals and groups that controlled how the factors were used to develop their impact on education. These people vied for power and created increasingly complex methods to convince others that their ideas were best. These individuals and groups can be known as the **ideological managers** of the evolution of American education. It is through the struggles between differing individuals and groups that we come to see which ideological managers prevailed during which era to determine what impact was felt in schools. These power players, then, had tremendous impact on American education within the five factors.

The factors spiral in and out of time. For example, during the comprehensive school movement of the 1880s and 1890s, the economic factor was monumental in influencing the school system to create jobs for industry. This development, in turn, influenced what was called the **differentiated curriculum**, which was used to sort and train individual students for particular factory jobs. The sorting and training of the differentiated curriculum was a form of **tracking** to establish social and economic levels or status of individuals. At the same time, this system had as its purpose the training of a workforce to be used as **human capital** for the country's economic status in the world. The same sort of tracking can be traced back to the 1600s and 1700s when only certain people were allowed to attend reading and writing schools, and others were allowed to attend Latin grammar schools. The intent of this separation was not so much to build America into a world power as it was to put people in their places in society. The tracking of the differentiated curriculum can be traced forward to today's version of tracking students in advanced placement or special education classes. This contemporary tracking can be seen as a social sorting, but its purpose could also be interpreted as training skilled workers and advanced workers for the United States' economic success.

Another example of the struggle for **ideological management** that impacted schools could be that of **dominant culture** status in America. As will be seen in Chapter 2 and thereafter, the American dominant culture was established when the first Europeans came to America in the early 1600s. Throughout history in every era, this dominant culture has asserted itself over all other cultures: the Native Americans who were here before the members of the dominant culture arrived; the Germans, French, Italians, Poles, and Irish who arrived later; and other immigrant cultures such as the Chinese, Japanese, Koreans, and Hmong, which developed over the years. This dominant culture could be viewed as the overriding ideological manager in the evolution of

Differentiated curriculum

A school curriculum design that allows for placing students into three or four different educational tracks

Tracking

The placement of students into curriculum tracks organized for specific organizational goals

Human capital

The term used to describe people trained to be workers in the American economy

Ideological management

The phrase used to describe the idea that whoever controls the knowledge controls the power

Dominant culture

The most populous and thus the most dominant culture in a society

American education. Clearly, the ideas of the dominant culture fashioned most of the essential elements of schooling in America through the centuries. Philosophical, religious, social, economic, and political factors all developed under the management of the dominant culture, and these factors played significant roles in the ideological management of schools. This dominant culture, almost 400 years later, still exists as it did when America first began and is still asserting its domain over schools and society via philosophical, religious, social, economic, and political influence. Brief contemporary examples include high-stakes testing and increased religious freedom in public schools. Social norms developed from single-culture points of view, economic divisions in the funding of equal education, and politicians creating laws and norms for schools. Though the specific issues have changed throughout the centuries, the ideological management has rarely come from anywhere other than the dominant culture.

This is not to say that there were not differing points of view within the dominant culture. Surely, American education has developed through a plethora of hard-fought educational battles over philosophical, religious, social, economic, and political issues. It is also not to say that the ideological managers always won clear-cut decisions for what has occurred in American society and schools. Clearly, ideas in all of the factors have been altered and massaged as they have been implemented on national, state, and local levels. For example, the Gary Plan (Mondale & Patton, 2001, pp. 78–96) for work/study was tremendously popular in pockets of the nation. In other areas of the nation, only parts of the plan were used. In still other places, the Gary Plan was not used at all. The ideological managers have often seen their victories reversed as well. For example, early in our history the rigidity and obedience orientation of the Lancaster model of classroom management gave way to the more child-centered ideas of Rousseau, Pestalozzi, Froebel, and others (Kaestle, 1983). Classroom management philosophy, theory, and practice have been reversed several times in the development of American education. These are examples of how, over the nation's history, there have been struggles for the ideological management of what occurs in American schools. These struggles form the essence of the nature of our system of education. They will continue.

This brief background illustrates what schools were like throughout history, and we can follow the train of thought that connects each era of history to the last and to the next to explain where we are in contemporary education. The logical progression of ideas—as society developed, new knowledge was gained, increased communication occurred, the population increased, and the nation developed—is fascinating to explore. The ideological management of one era evolved right into ensuing eras. Further, ideas were recycled over decades and centuries by new ideological managers who tweaked them or viewed them to be used in altered ways. This is much more an evolution of ideas than a simple "been there, done that" reaction to educational development. Cooperative learning, for example, is not just group work (Johnson & Johnson, 1997). To see the ideas in new ways because of new events, new knowledge, and new ways of thinking is a tribute to the leaders who have guided education. Thus, we examine the ideological managers via five primary factors in order to understand their impact on American schools and explain the development and evolution of education in America.

The question becomes how we should study the evolution of American education. How should we go about seeking this knowledge? The answer is to seek knowledge with emotional compassion and intensity of intellectual endeavor. If we sit back unemotionally and simply read the facts about people, places, events, and times, we will miss the joy and understanding of emotional and intellectual connections throughout history that have driven us to where we are and where we will be going. We will miss the shaping of our nation and its schools and

the compassion and struggle that went into it. We'll miss the depth of what it means to develop a system of education by analyzing the motives behind the ideas of the ideological managers and the reasons why people accepted or rejected these ideas. Therefore, we need to approach our study with compassion for what has evolved and understanding of what it meant and still means for us—then, now, and into the future. We must embrace the events of our history, react emotionally to what it means to us, and intellectualize the meaning of what has happened. Then we must interact with others in the same manner to arrive at new emotions and new understanding as we see the evolution of American education through differing frames of reference. With this new understanding comes the emotional power of human existence and the excitement of intellectual challenge.

This primer is an overview in that it offers a broad look at the unfolding of the evolution of American educational history. In that sense, I hope that the reader will come away with a clear comprehension of the main factors of how education has become what it has become. For some it will provide a substantial understanding of the topic, one worthy of reading and knowing. For others, it will solidify previous knowledge and make connections to what they already know. Perhaps depth will be added to previous knowledge. For still others, it will provide stimulation for further studying of the evolution of American education in areas they had not previously approached. Questions at the end of chapters are provided to stimulate discussion more than for actual review. Selected topics for further study are included also to pique interest in topics surrounding the chapter and to lead to further study topics on the development of American education.

Glossary

Basic Principles—The expectation of citizens in the New England colonies to be God-fearing, father-obeying, and law-abiding.

Differentiated Curriculum—A school curriculum design that allows for placing students into three or four tracks in order to train them to work in American industry as human capital.

Divine Intervention—The belief that God directs human lives.

Dominant Culture—The most populous and thus the most dominant culture in a society.

Evolution of American Education—The connected development through primary factors of the American system of education from its beginnings in the 1630s to the present.

Good Society—The society expected to result from living according to the basic principles.

Human Capital—The term used to describe people trained to be workers in the American economy.

Ideological Management—The term meant to describe the idea that whoever controls the knowledge controls the power.

Ideological Managers—The individuals and groups who have controlled the ideas that have influenced and shaped the evolution of American education through the primary factors.

Primary Factors—The philosophical, religious, social, economic, and political factors that have heavily influenced the evolution of American education.

Religious Persecution—Depriving individuals and groups of their right to practice and espouse the religion of their choice.

Tracking—The placement of students into curriculum tracks organized for specific educational goals.

American Education Through the Civil War

Instruments of religion

The term is used to describe schools as vehicles for teaching religious indoctrination

Common school movement

A school model in the nineteenth century that sought to bring together White children in a common school to perpetuate the goals of the then dominant White culture

American schools began as **instruments of religion**. When Jonathan Winthrop and his followers first arrived in the 1620s, there was no time to build schools. They were trying to build a republic of God-fearing citizens. While men and older boys were out in the fields, women taught children to read the Bible and write the scriptures. Strict adherence to the Bible, which saw women as nurturers, resulted in women teaching themselves to read and write and then assuming responsibility to nurture their children's moral growth by teaching the scriptures to them. This arrangement foreshadowed the establishment of women as the backbone of American education, a trend seen in the **common school movement** and one which continues today. It also established the religious nature of American education. Under the Protestant theology carried over from Europe, early schools began to develop in the wilderness of our country. Though French, German, Dutch, and other populations were present, the first

formal schools began as English-speaking schools in what is known as the **Massachusetts Bay Colony**. The White, Protestant ideological managers of this era sought to create a moral, God-fearing society. There were three goals of major importance for the establishment of the good society in the good republic. All people were to:

1. Honor, fear, and obey God.
2. Honor, fear, and obey the father in the home.
3. Honor, fear, and obey the government. (Spring, 2001a, pp. 11–17)

These basic tenets came from within the Protestant Calvinistic philosophy. **Calvinism** is the belief that humans are born in sin and must purge this sin as children grow into adults. Stated another way, Calvinism could be described as being born with the devil and needing to drive the devil out. Religious indoctrination and social norm factors joined to promote politically motivated laws in 1642 and 1647 that created schooling along the lines of Protestant theology. These two laws, the **Massachusetts Law of 1642** and **the Old Deluder Satan Law of 1647**, became the first major educational laws. The Law of 1642 called for all parents to find someone to teach their children how to read the Bible, write out scriptures, follow Protestant theology, and obey the laws of the land. The Old Deluder Satan Law of 1647 called for all towns of 50 households or more to appoint a teacher to teach reading and writing and all towns of 100 or more households to build a school and hire a schoolmaster. The first schools were created mainly as a result of these laws in order to form a republic of common values and allegiances. In this form of republicanism, we can see the beginnings of formal schooling in America (Hlebowitsh, 2001, pp. 180–181).

The First Schools

Though there were several names for early schools (dame schools, petty schools, town schools, Sunday schools, pay schools, people's colleges), the types of

---

Massachusetts Bay Colony

The seventeenth-century Puritan settlement in New England that sought religious freedom and economic independence

---

Calvinism

A philosophy associated with the Protestant theology of the Puritans that taught that humans were born in sin

---

Massachusetts Law of 1642 and the Old Deluder Satan Law of 1647

They are considered the first two major laws in the evolution of American educational history

schools that existed in this era can be summarized in three ways. One type was the reading and writing schools for non-college-bound, non-leadership-bound students. The curriculum of these schools was simply reading and writing and a small amount of ciphering. Often these were actually two different schools—one for reading and one for writing. Latin grammar schools were created for college-bound (Harvard, 1636) and leadership-bound (politicians) students. These schools had an organized curriculum of seven years which featured Latin, Greek, and Hebrew (Webb, 2006, p. 6). These schools were sometimes looked upon as finishing schools of **ornamental knowledge** for the privileged (Nash, 2005, p. 42). Apprenticeship schools were created for those heading for specific trades. These were situations in which students might live with another family for a while to get training in a specific skill or occupation. Very few girls attended school, and those who did were found in the reading and writing schools or, even more rarely, in apprenticeship schools. Girls were allowed to attend only when boys were not present, usually before or after school or during the summer when boys were working (Kaestle, 1983, p. 28).

All schools were based on the religious belief in the need to read the Bible and write out scriptures in order to lead a moral, God-fearing (and thus virtuous) life. The Calvinist philosophy was the bedrock of school and society. The Massachusetts Bay Colony exemplified Protestant theology. It is interesting to note that, in addition to the Protestant beliefs (fearing and obeying God, the father in the home, and the government), the colony also included seven other specific purposes for schools. Remarkably, these purposes can be traced as goals from that time forward throughout history. In fact, their social, economic, political, and religious importance escalated and resulted in many educational laws that impacted school programs over time. They were the following:

1. End crime
2. Eliminate poverty

Ornamental knowledge
Information taught in the seventeenth and eighteenth centuries such as etiquette or how to be a gentleman

3. Provide equality of opportunity
4. Improve the economy
5. Train workers
6. Create social stability
7. Create political stability (Spring, 2001a, p. 10)

These education policies of the Massachusetts Bay Colony are considered precursors to the development of public schooling in the United States in the early nineteenth century.

As the colonies expanded, differing forms of schooling philosophy developed, and, as a result, regional differences came about. Historians most often focus on the New England Colonies with its government and religious involvement in education. The Middle Colonies developed parochial schools with no government involvement while education in the Southern Colonies was all about social class and did not include government or even the church (Murphy, 2006, pp. 214–218).

Between 1630 and 1642 over 20,000 Puritans came to the Massachusetts Bay Colony (Webb, 2006, p. 68). These well-educated English Puritans valued education and desired to establish it quickly in the New World. Aside from the rigidity of Calvinistic theology regarding obedience, the Puritans' educational philosophy included the education necessary for religious instruction and salvation and the belief that economic self-reliance by literate people must result. At first the Puritans wanted to copy England by having wealthy elites pay for schools, but the scarcity of wealthy people in the New World and the fear that their children might not get a Puritan education caused them to consider a more direct role for the state (Webb, 2006, p. 69).

Colonial schoolmasters ranged from widows or housewives in dame schools to college-educated masters in grammar schools. Most teachers were men who did not intend to make teaching their career. Often these men were waiting to get into the ministry, or they were ministers earning extra

income. Some teachers were people who had failed at other professions, and some were moonlighters from night jobs. Most teachers were chosen by locals because of their religious beliefs, and often teachers were viewed as assistant pastors. At the same time, teachers were commonly believed to be ignorant and unstable, a perception resulting from the fact that some were actually indentured servants working off their passage to the New World. Surprisingly, teachers often taught in foreign languages. There were many variations of school years and school daily schedules; seasonal work predicted when school was in session and what hours it would meet (Webb, 2006, pp. 92–94).

Stretching: 1723–1830

This era brought about dramatic change as some leaders of the country challenged the prevailing Puritan ideological managers. New ideas, sometimes referred to as the Intellectual Revolution, were spawned by **Cato's Letters** and brought to the fore later by Thomas Jefferson. *Cato's Letters* were anonymous publications circulated throughout the country between 1720 and 1723 by Thomas Gordon and John Trenchard. Reprinted for 25 years, these letters are sometimes referred to as the beginning of the American Revolution (Spring, 2001a, pp. 22–24). Gordon and Trenchard were not as much against the rigid biblical curriculum of schools, noted for their strict discipline, as they were in favor of a loosening of the rigidity, especially in the areas of thought, speech, and the press. They defined the freedom of thought and speech as a right that can be abridged only to protect the rights of others. By the 1760s, Jefferson challenged the notion that education should only be rote memorization of the Bible to mold children into obedient servers of God, father, and government. Jefferson and his followers wanted more freedoms, specifically the freedoms of thought, speech, and the press. Jefferson believed freedom and liberty would lead people down the road to progress and happiness; thus, they would also lead the nation

Cato's Letters

A series of anonymously published letters from 1720 to 1723 declaring the desire for increased individual rights in the colonies

to progress and happiness. Jefferson's ideas regarding newspapers being more important than schools exemplifies the point. Jefferson thought that schooling should neither impose political values nor mold virtuous citizens. Jefferson and his followers abided by the strict religious, philosophical, social, and political factors that had been set up by the early ideological managers, but they wanted to broaden them for more personal freedom and growth. They were willing to include the already established moral, God-fearing education along with what was called "education for virtue" for future leadership. They desired more curriculum than just the Bible and more experiences than just learning obedience. The rigidity of order and God-fearing obedience was combined with the quest for more individual freedoms. This expansion of the school's role resulted in the broadening of school curricula to include more subjects such as mathematics, geography, and cartography.

The Balance of Freedom and Order

New England Primer
The major textbook for American schools in the eighteenth and nineteenth centuries

Patriotic Americans
An eighteenth- and nineteenth-century term meant to create a citizenry separate from European influence

Unified national spirit
The concept to create a patriotic American national unity by establishing school curricula based on American cultural features, such as songs, celebrations, or holidays

Noah Webster might be described as one of the most ambitious patriots of early American history. He was so adamant about breaking away from England that he wrote and published a three-volume collection that replaced the original post-Bible text in use in American schools, the **New England Primer**. Webster's collection was entitled *A Grammatical Institute of the English Language*. The first volume taught spelling, the second taught grammar, and the third taught reading. Webster took the moral and academic teachings of the *New England Primer* and organized them further to establish an American culture separate from England. His books were meant to produce good, **patriotic Americans**, to develop an American language, and to create a **unified national spirit**. He wanted to build nationalism through an emotional patriotism—a citizenry willing to die for its country. He urged the establishment and teaching of a solely nationalistic curriculum which emphasized national songs and celebrations, national holidays, and the teaching of only American authors. Webster was a Calvinist, especially regarding the discipline and obedience needed to mold children into God-fearing, law-abiding citizens. To this end, he established moral and federal catechisms designed to keep children in line by requiring them to recite memorized questions and answers that would indicate their obedience to God and to their country. Webster's ideas reflected the cultural beliefs of the time and had a major effect on children's education in the eighteenth and nineteenth centuries. His ideas symbolized the rejection of a multicultural society and the establishment of an English-speaking Protestant culture (Schuman, 2004, pp. 53–55).

Webster believed that Jefferson's ideas of freedom would create chaos out of serenity. He argued against Jefferson but was forced to compromise because of the popularity of the ideas in *Cato's Letters*. The arguments between Jefferson's and Webster's ideas resulted in what is known as the balance of freedom and order. A compromise was reached based primarily on political factors. Jefferson and Webster agreed that more freedoms could be incorporated as long as the focus on education for virtue remained. This ideological compromise basically meant that education could result in a broader range of learning experiences but was still meant to create virtuous citizens to serve the nation in moral, God-fearing ways. It could also be added that it meant, Anglo-American, Protestant, White, wealthy, male ways, for these were the people leading the development of American society, building and running the schools, and determining the curriculum. These were the ideological managers. These were also the people who could afford to send their sons to school. This dominant culture of people was creating the first laws and social norms of the country in its own image.

Schools continued to be philosophically Calvinistic but became more open to education beyond rote memorization of the Bible. For example, academies were developed to teach both orna-

Utilitarian (useful) knowledge

Skills taught in the eighteenth and nineteenth centuries directly related to occupational skills, such as carpentry or accounting

mental (status) knowledge and **utilitarian (useful) knowledge**. Ornamental knowledge came to include such social skills as knowledge, etiquette, reading, and debate. Utilitarian knowledge referred to practical working skills such as blacksmithing, carpentry, and animal husbandry for home and occupation. In the 1740s and 1750s Ben Franklin became the leading proponent for utilitarian schools, called academies (Nash, 2005, p. 42). These schools escalated the efforts of reading and writing schools, Latin grammar schools, and apprenticeship schools to include not only religious, social, and political orientation but also preparation for employment. Frequently fathers would have to send their sons away to boarding schools for a fee. The academies were governed by a variety of public and private groups and evolved in divergent ways over the next several decades, sometimes being called small colleges and at other times being called high schools. By the end of the century, they became identified as secondary education for the elite. Girls were allowed to attend academies but were taught in separate rooms or buildings at different times of the day or year (Kaestle, 1983, p. 28). Female academies began between 1780 and 1840 but were renamed female seminaries later on the way to higher education for women. Though born out of a need for practical skills, freedom of thought, and freedom of speech, these academies came about primarily to confirm social status for elite members of society (Nash, 2005, pp. 35–52).

School Organization

At this time hierarchies began to develop regarding the organization and control of schools. By now there were increasing numbers of schoolhouses in the villages and around the countryside. County supervisors and—when urban areas developed—city supervisors, eventually known as superintendents, were responsible for creating a school curriculum. They would travel to schools to make sure the curriculum was being followed. As attendance increased, the local schoolmarms needed assistance, and thus addi-

tional teachers were hired. The original teacher would then be considered a lead or principal teacher. From this the bureaucracy of schools began to develop, adding the many layers seen in today's schools.

As schools became more popular, the increase in attendance also led to new thinking regarding school and classroom management. One of the popular leaders emerging along these lines was Joseph Lancaster, who created what is called a **monitorial system** (Kaestle, 1983, p. 41). Many school leaders, especially DeWitt Clinton in New York, were popularizing the Lancasterian model. This model, with its emphasis on nationalism, obedience, and order, fit well with the popular beliefs of the time. It included student helpers, called monitors, who would help a lead teacher deliver the lessons of the day. This system accommodated the teaching of large classes. Mottos such as *Let there be no idle moments!* and *Everything has its place and everything in it!* were meant to create order and obedience, self-discipline, and proper habits. Lancaster, who advocated a reward and punishment philosophy, called submission, order, and obedience the civic virtues and wanted schools to run like well-oiled machines.

What was once a struggling republic was now a nation. An even bigger push toward nationalism developed not only in society but also in schools. If the purpose of education before the Revolution was to confer social status and to lead children to live a Godly life, educational purpose after the Revolution was to build nationalism, shape good citizens, and reform society (Spring, 2001a, p. 32).

Monitorial system
A system of school management and instruction that incorporated the use of student helpers to teach other students

Segregated Education and the Birth of the Modern Public School: 1830–1895

This era found the ideological managers of the dominant culture fighting to maintain their control on many fronts. A new country had emerged, and unification was a major issue. The leaders in society were pushing for unification via common school ideology. Thus, the common school movement dominated

education in this era. The goals of the common school movement, most notably professed by Horace Mann, were to educate all school-going children in a common school with a common social/political curriculum. Though the predecessors of these schools had indoctrinated students to obey the government, it was at this time that schools were first recognized as the official purveyors of the government's will. The key to creating a good society was using the schools to do so. Mann wanted to use local taxes to pay for state controlled schools that pushed a national agenda. Though the push for **national unity** was roundly supported, local taxation and state control were not. Nevertheless, the common school curriculum developed into a social/political shaping of students. The three distinctive aspects of the common school movement were the emphasis on educating all children in a common school house to solve social problems and build a political community; the idea of using **schools as an instrument of government policy** and thus creating a direct linkage between educators, government policy, and social/political/economic reform; and the creation of state agencies to control local schools in carrying out state and national goals (Kaestle, 1983, p. 61).

Although Calvinism was not totally abandoned, a new philosophy using the concept of the **blank slate** was adopted. This philosophy, taken from John Locke, allowed the schools to determine that children knew little to nothing and could be socially and politically indoctrinated by the teachers' writing out of the government's curriculum on the students' **blank slates** (minds). This highly nationalistic curriculum fostered the unification that the ideological managers desired. Later, this nationalistic approach would evolve into **100% Americanization** programs in both schools and society. The entire school experience was set up to promote the values of the Anglo-American, Protestant, White, wealthy male: the dominant culture that had been clearly established from the beginning in American society and education. Common school devices such as the

National unity
The push by American schools in the nineteenth century to be independent of the influence of other nations

Schools as an instrument of government policy
School curricula's focus on political and primary factors rather than religion

Blank slate
The aspect of Lockean philosophy that refers to humans as being born without knowledge and thus having blank slates for schools to fill with learning

100% Americanization
The plethora of programs meant to promote the values of the dominant culture in schools and society at large early in the nineteenth century

Webster's American Dictionary of the English Language

A major source for the Americanization of the English language in the nineteenth century

use of only nationalistic literature, the use of ***Webster's American Dictionary of the English Language,*** the use of ***McGuffey's Readers***, and the use of other dominant culture literature were combined with the use of patriotic songs, dances, anthems, and allegiances, to promote a national unity through the dominant culture's value structure.

Women: The Ideal Teachers

McGuffey's Readers

A school text created for the common school movement devised to promote national unity

This era featured many other influences on American schools. One of the most significant was the identification and recruitment of women as ideal teachers. This choice comes as no surprise as women were thought of as having a particular place in the home and in society. Now their particular place would lead them to teaching. Women were teachers of their own children right from the start. In addition, women had to teach themselves to read even before teaching their children, and hence women were viewed as having natural learning, teaching, and nurturing abilities. Having studied the Bible most thoroughly, as was their place to do, women were looked upon as moral guideposts. From the 1600s to the common school movement, women proved themselves in all of these ways. By the time of the common schools, teacher institutes and normal schools were established, most notably by Emma Willard and Samuel T. Hall, to train women not only in pedagogy but also in the moral and virtuous upbringing of America's children. Not only did this development mark the beginning of the study of pedagogy, but it purported to deliver children from evil through the teaching of character education. Johann Pestalozzi, Jean-Jacques Rousseau, and Frederick Froebel all contributed to the ideas of **republican motherhood** (a term created by Benjamin Rush to mean linking the domestic role of women with the development of republican citizens) and the maternal model of instruction (the concept used to replace the intellectual overseer and drillmaster concept of classroom teaching) (Nash, 2005, p. 27). Women were thought to be ideal nurturers and teachers as

Republican motherhood

The idea that suggests the expansion of mothers' roles beyond the family

opposed to men who were considered not nearly as moral, patient, educated, or stable as women. In addition, women were considered symbols of charity and as such were expected to and be willing to work for little or no pay. All of these factors led to women being looked upon as the natural teachers for American schools. Of course, one of the many reasons women wanted to become teachers was that no other professions or occupations were open to women outside the home. Thus, many women were eager to participate in a meaningful endeavor which provided opportunities for growth and independence.

Juxtaposed against the popularity of the works of Pestalozzi, Rousseau, and Froebel in the common school movement was the widespread use of the Joseph Lancaster-driven monitorial system of school management. This rigid, Bible-based, authoritarian method of teaching in schools led to a standard indoctrination for national unity and a strict demand for obedience. As early as 1805, Lancaster described his schools as running like a well-oiled machine: like a factory. This description foreshadowed the upcoming work of Frederick W. Taylor during the Industrial Revolution. Lancaster's system was based on rewards and punishments, emphasizing the virtues of submission, order, and industriousness. These were popular themes of the time and would continue as mainstays beyond the common school movement.

Native Americans and African Americans

Native Americans had been treated as heathens and savages since the early 1600s. Americans such as John Eliot, George Washington, Thomas Jefferson, Thomas L. McKenney, and Andrew Jackson, among many others, had been attempting to assimilate or eliminate Native Americans for 200 years via a variety of different plans to acquire their land and deculturalize them. One plan was the early missionary teaching of Christianity by John Eliot and his followers, who had planned to convert Native Americans to Christianity in order to reform their so-called heathen ways. Clearly, the Native American ethics

of living were not in concert with the Puritan Protestant values. The Protestants believed that hard work and the accumulation of property provided protection against sin and stopped the mind from wandering. They thought the accumulation of wealth was a sign of God's blessing. Native Americans believed in sharing property, food, and time. The accumulation of property was not important, and Native Americans had no conception of work being intrinsically good. Therefore, Christianizing Native Americans became important to White people. Later, in 1819 the Civilization Act was passed due greatly to the efforts of the Superintendent of Indian Trade, Thomas L. McKenney. He promoted tribal schools taught by White missionaries to Christianize Native Americans to "civilize" them. Washington, Jefferson, and others created elaborate plans through which they hoped to influence Native Americans to become economic consumers who would need to sell their land to support this consumption. President Jackson, military generals, and others wanted to wage war and either remove Native Americans to the West or kill them.

Deculturalization

Stripping away others' culture by preventing them from speaking their language or adhering to their customs, traditions, celebrations, religion, and education

To varying degrees, all of these efforts worked. With the usual techniques of **deculturalization** (taking away language, culture, traditions, celebrations, religion, and education), these tactics came to a head with the Indian Removal Act of 1830 and the ensuing Trail of Tears, which were justified by several federal court decisions and the idea of manifest destiny, but were mostly seen as the enforcement of the dominating culture's will. By 1858, the United States had developed reservations and on-reservation boarding schools. By 1868, the Indian Peace Commission established the goal of teaching all Native Americans English. By 1889, off-reservation boarding schools began with the Carlisle Indian School in Carlisle, Pennsylvania. Interestingly, the campus of that original off-reservation boarding school is now the home of the War College and is used for military instruction. Land allotment programs for Native Americans were established to

instill capitalistic values by means of the Dawes Bill of 1887. In 1889, Americanization programs replaced Native American culture in Indian schools. This removal of Indian tribes from the Southeast to west of the Mississippi in the 1830s was indicative of a trend. The Native Americans were removed, slaughtered, and pushed aside until the 1960s when they began to regain some of their rights.

Other dominated cultures suffered the same fate as the Native Americans. African Americans, who fought to advance from no education at all to inferior, segregated education, continued to struggle against domination in this era. Southern Blacks established oral traditions of song and dance while Northern Blacks attempted political challenges for the rights to be free and educated. Southern enslaved Blacks contributed music and stories of oppression and focused on literacy, citizenship, education, and jobs. Northern free Blacks struggled for educational opportunity and focused on literacy, political actions, and judicial decisions. In both cases, efforts were futile as African Americans were simply looked upon only as slaves for White people.

From 1830 until the Civil War, segregated education was the only option for African Americans aside from what was in some cases substantial home schooling. African Americans were prevented from attending White schools in the eighteenth century, but by 1806 Boston had set up and partially funded segregated schools. By 1820, these schools were recognized as inferior to White schools in terms of buildings, educational level of teachers, materials, and maintenance. Against odds, African Americans established a segregated school system, albeit weak and disconnected, on their own. In 1849, the Roberts Case continued to support segregated schools (Kaestle, 1983, pp. 178–180). Ben Roberts lost his bid to have his daughter attend a nearby school for White children. Still, by the beginning of the Civil War, 4,000 Blacks attended school in slave states, and 23,000 Blacks attended in free states. Some Blacks also went to Europe to be educated (Webb, 2006, p. 197). With

the Emancipation Proclamation in 1863, African Americans escalated not only their dreams for freedom and civil rights, but their dreams for equal education.

However, progress was slow, and segregated schools continued to be the norm after 1863 with increased attendance and involvement by African Americans and some White philanthropists. Of particular note was the work of Mary Peake in developing and building many schools throughout this era. A push for Black education in the South occurred during and right after the Civil War. During Reconstruction (1865–1877), hundreds of teachers flocked to the South to teach freed slaves. Offering significant financial assistance toward these efforts were the Peabody Fund, Slater Fund, the Anna T. Jeanes Fund, the Julius Rosenwald Fund, the General Education Board, and the Freedman's Bureau. By the 1870s, with Southerners believing that the expansion of education was necessary for industrializing the South, Blacks increased their attendance in school enough to outnumber Whites attending school. Seen as cheap labor, Blacks were kept on low rungs of the education and the economic systems. By 1900 Whites had re-established 54% of the population attending schools, while Blacks were reduced to 31% in order to not take space from White children (Webb, 2006, p. 200). Of note were Booker T. Washington and W. E. B. Du Bois. Though the work of Washington was controversial, he was seen as the leading voice for African Americans until his death in 1915, when Du Bois assumed the leadership. Their almost opposite views of education aroused controversy in their era and continue to do so today. Their publications, *Up From Slavery* (Washington, 1901) and *The Souls of Black Folk: Essays and Sketches* (Du Bois, 1903) espoused their beliefs and argued their differences. Nevertheless, they both wanted equality of educational, economic, and social opportunity for all Americans, including African Americans. It would take another generation for significant change to begin to occur for African Americans (Webb, 2006, pp. 197–201).

Asian Americans and Mexican Americans

Asian populations and Mexican populations suffered the same fate as Native Americans and African Americans under the White dominant culture and determined minority deculturalization techniques. The "yellow peril" idea of Asian Americans taking White jobs, along with the common notion of White supremacy, was the motivation to perform the usual deculturalization techniques on Asian Americans. Chinese immigrants first came to America in the 1840s and 1850s to work and earn money in the California gold mines. Their intent was to work the mines to earn some money and then return to China. By 1860, 16,000 Chinese immigrants were stranded in America. When the mining ran out, many Chinese found themselves without enough money to return to China. They took jobs at one-third to two-thirds the rate of pay of White people and worked in agricultural fields and at building the Transcontinental Railroad. Racial hostility mounted as the Chinese were accused of taking jobs from White people. Japanese immigrants began to arrive in the late 1860s and into the 1870s, 1880s, and 1890s. They found jobs as planters and in the silk industry. Both the Chinese and the Japanese (and later Koreans) were denied citizenship under the Naturalization Law of 1870, which re-interpreted the 1790 Naturalization Law to mean that only White people could be citizens. Asians were not considered White. School codes of the 1870s and 1880s excluded immigrants, declaring that schools should educate all White children. The Page Law (1875) forbade immigration of Asian laborers and was followed by the 1882 Chinese Exclusion Act, which allowed only merchants, students, teachers, and diplomats to immigrate. The Mamie Tape decision in 1885, a decision in favor of equal education, resulted in additional laws passed to establish Chinese segregated education. Though not on as large a scale as African Americans, Asian Americans began establishing their own segregated schools. The African American and Asian American quest for equal schooling led to the establishment of segregated schools for minority populations. It was too early in America's development, still, for equality to occur (Spring, 2001b, pp. 55–66).

"Keeping them on their knees" was one of the concepts that explained Mexican Americans being coerced out of schools and into the fields to do the manual labor for wealthier White farmers. Mexican Americans, like Native Americans, Asian Americans, and African Americans, had to overcome social, political, and economic factors to arrive at any education for their children, much less equal education. Suffice it to say, education was not equal during the time of the common school movement as the wealthier White dominant culture solidified its ideas for national unity. The Treaty of Guadalupe Hidalgo (1848) raised the issue of what should happen to Mexicans living in the land ceded to the United States following the Mexican American War (1845–1848). Though they were claimed as citizens eventually (a notion that was resented by most Mexicans), they were subject to segregated schooling. As in the other ethnic minority populations, economic exploitation of Mexicans was justified for the most part by racism. Not welcome in public schools, Mexicans were forced to work in the fields and on the railroads as cheap labor while attending private and parochial schools when they could. In the 1880s attempts were made to establish Mexican schools in Texas and California. The plight of Mexican Americans symbolized a major problem confronted by White Americans in their dealings with all ethnic minority cultures. Although Whites wanted to keep minorities out of school for economic exploitation, they knew that the best way to Americanize them was to keep them in school. It would take minority populations another hundred years to begin realizing substantial gains.

The Irish Catholics

One dominated culture that did make significant strides during the common school movement was

the population of Irish Catholics. Arriving in the late 1830s and early 1840s, millions of Irish Catholics came to America, many for the same reason Winthrop and his followers did, to escape religious persecution. They were met at the shores with horrendous humiliation by Protestant Whites, the dominant culture, who accused them of coming to America to destroy the American Protestant faith. The Irish Catholics were seen as both a religious and an economic threat. They were accused of acting on passion rather than reason. They were called superstitious and were associated with Satan. They were called names, among those mongrels and devils, and were told not to apply for jobs and to go home (Spring, 2001a, pp. 87–92).

Irish Americans persevered despite enormous discrimination. After recognizing the Protestant philosophy underlying the common school movement, especially in the use of the King James Version of the Bible, Catholic youths stopped attending school. They viewed school as anti-Catholic, citing stories and language that were offensive to their religious beliefs. As a result, these youths were unemployed and subject to delinquency and gang affiliation. Adults, understanding the problem, attempted to establish Catholic education in a dual system of education. When that effort failed, they tried to take religion out of the common school. Both ideas were met with vehement opposition. In spite of the support of the powerful Bishop Hughes and Governor Seward of New York in 1838, many Irish were beaten and killed in the 1842 Bible Riots. Feeling the weight of the Anglo-American, Protestant-oriented school curriculum and the resulting disfranchisement of their children, the Irish Catholics established what we now know as the parochial school system via the **Plenary Councils** (Kaestle, 1983, pp. 166–171). After social, political, and economic upheaval that in some cases led to violence, the Irish Catholics split from the common school movement and created their own schools. Thus, the common school movement never became what it was intended to be: a common

Plenary Councils

The sequence of three meetings in the nineteenth century by Irish Catholic leaders to devise a plan to educate Irish Catholics, which triggered the beginning of a parochial school system of education

school for all. It never achieved its goal of an education for all people of all social, economic, political, religious classes. In fact, the common school movement drove deeper wedges into American society (Webb, 2006, pp. 155–156).

Irish Catholics: The Uncommon in Common Public Schools, 1825–1890

Perhaps no other group of immigrants felt the sting of discrimination more acutely than did the Irish Catholics. Their story of immigration and subsequent involvement in the American educational system is rich with righteous attempts to overcome what the Irish Catholics perceived as a deliberate and vicious attack on their religion and ethnic background. They left Ireland for a variety of reasons, but they came to America uniformly thinking of one dual concept: freedom and opportunity. Their expectations were met with an astounding resistance that surprised and disillusioned the Irish Catholics who immigrated to the eastern shores of America. Stunned at first, Irish Catholics would soon realize that in order to save their heritage, they would need to take a stand in support of their religious and educational rights in the still new nation called the United States. This Irish Catholic assertion of social/civil rights would change the American educational system forever.

As the Irish Catholics began arriving in the harbors of New York, Boston, Philadelphia, and Baltimore in the 1820s, 1830s, and 1840s, they had high hopes for a new life in America that would help them forget about the miserable lives most of them had been living in Ireland. Clearly, by the 1830s, the Irish Catholics were an oppressed population in their own homeland. The Irish Catholics only owned about 14% of the land (Spring, 2001a, p. 87). The dominant culture of Ireland, which consisted mostly of non-Catholic English descendants, forced the Irish Catholics to live in extremely poor housing. This housing usually consisted of run-down huts that were poorly built near fruitless land that had various problems of tillage, terrain, and irrigation. The land

contributed to a lack of food for the Irish Catholics, which in turn made for a dreary, unhealthy, and unhappy existence. These circumstances were enough for some of the Irish Catholics to begin to plan a trip to America where they thought freedom and opportunity were waiting for them. Perhaps what the Irish did not realize was that American colonists, by and large, were themselves immigrants, and, like the Irish, they were themselves European immigrants. Unfortunately for the Irish, the American colonists were European immigrants from England. This, of course, was the same England which had long dominated Ireland. In Ireland, the English had looked upon the Irish as savages and animals. They had no respect for them as human beings. The Irish were thought to be slaves of their passions. They were thought to be the "drunken Irish"—emotional, superstitious, unpredictable, and untrustworthy. They were said to enjoy the "low pleasures" too much (Schuman, 2004, p. 62). In short, the Irish were not on a level with European non-Catholics. As these same European non-Catholics settled in America, the same stereotypes were adopted by the American dominant culture and were used to place Irish Catholics at the lowest level of American society.

By 1845, a million Irish had immigrated to America to escape the miserable life they had lived in Ireland (Spring, 2001a, p. 87). By 1847, 37,000 Irish immigrants were living in Boston alone (Schuman, 2004, p. 62). In addition to the inequity in land ownership, poor housing, and poor food supply, many Irish Catholics came to America to escape the religious persecution they felt by the Protestant Church of England, which had become the dominant religion of Ireland. The potato famine, which began in 1845, was yet another reason for the Irish to seek freedom and opportunity in America. To escape starvation, another 1.5 million Irish came to America (Spring, 2001a, p. 87). Arriving at the great port cities, especially New York and Boston, the Irish would soon realize that the New World might not be what they had expected.

Almost before they trooped down the plank off the ship after a difficult journey across the ocean, the Irish could sense the feeling of those on the shore who waited for their arrival. Carrying signs that would become only too familiar for the Irish, people on the docks welcomed the Irish to America with open hostility. Placards with ethnic slurs were held up in open view as the Irish came down the planks. More signs telling the Irish to go back to Ireland were accompanied by jeers and ethnic insults. Even more signs declaring "Irish Need Not Apply" told the Irish that Americans did not want them taking their jobs or their living quarters. These signs, shouts, and jeers would portend the difficulty the Irish would face in trying to work and live in their new land of freedom and opportunity. With this unexpected and hellish welcome, the Irish immigrants walked off their ship planks, onto dockside, and into another very difficult life. Their journey to the land of freedom and opportunity did not start out as they expected it would. At first blush, they did not appear to be any better off than they were in the land they had left. These Irish immigrants who were looked down upon in Ireland as the dregs of Irish society were now indoctrinated into their new role as dregs of American society. Upon their arrival, they were immediately slotted to the American bottom class in spite of the reality that the Irish immigrants were a "select, especially highly motivated, and unusually literate portion of Irish society" (Schuman, 2004, p. 62).

Over the course of history, the Irish have proven themselves to be a determined group and have established a record of survival during difficult times. In America their determination and survival skills began with their obtaining jobs building roads, working in mines, digging canals, and working on the railroads. They competed with other minority cultures, for example, African Americans, to get these positions. With the dominant culture keeping African Americans at the lowest rung of the economic and social ladders and treating them as property, animals, and slaves, the Irish joined them in the eyes of the

White Anglo-Saxon Protestant male dominant culture in America. Thus, European Americans thought
Irish Catholics should also be considered mere property to be used as slaves to fulfill the most difficult
and lowest level jobs. Irish Catholics were called
Irish dogs, dray horses, Irish slaves, and, perhaps
the worst, Irish niggers. Even folk songs of the time
laughed at these stereotypes and perpetuated the discrimination. However, it was not just jobs and the
lust for power, control, and domination that made
the dominant culture keep the Irish in check. There
was another reason lurking in the background of con-
sciousness that played an immense part in explain-
ing the dominant culture's planned, orchestrated, and
overt abuse of the Irish Catholics who had come to
America to escape oppression in Europe.

It was true that the dominant culture feared
that the Irish would take their jobs. This was a common complaint against all minority populations in
America. White people feared the "yellow peril" of
Asian immigrants taking their jobs. They also created
the "keep them on their knees (and out of schools)"
philosophy toward Hispanics, Latinos, and Mexican
immigrants in order to be sure that only the dirtiest,
most difficult jobs would be given to those populations so that they could serve White people's needs
with no chance of education or higher employment. American history also chronicles the incred-
ibly oppressive response to Native Americans and
African Americans, who were brutalized to reduce
their populations, isolated in geographic locations,
and made slaves to the dominant culture with little
to no hope for uplift in education or employment.
It was also true that the dominant culture did not
want the Irish Catholics taking their living quarters. Again, as this was true for all oppressed populations who throughout history have been forced to
live in substandard housing (huts, reservations, slave
houses), Irish immigrants were forced to live in the
substandard housing of urban ghettos. Overcrowded,
unsanitary, unsafe, and unhealthy housing was the
norm for Irish immigrants in their first 100 years in

America. With the Irish Catholics, however, in addition to the dominant culture's fear of job loss and housing loss, there was also the fear of Catholicism. In Europe, the English had freed the Catholics to become Christian, and, after the Church of England became Protestant, most Irish remained Catholic (Spring, 2001a, p. 87). Catholicism became a source of fear because the Protestant dominant culture came to believe that the Catholic Church was the church of Satan. In this regard, the minority religion was feared in the same way that minority ethnic cultures were feared; that is, the dominant culture wanted to protect their way of life and their own ethnic culture from those who were different. The Protestants in America went so far as to create stories that the Pope had sent the Irish Catholics to America to destroy the Protestant Church. Of greater impact than employment or housing, religion would become the most volatile aspect of the Irish Catholic presence in America and would directly affect the development of American education.

Common School Arguments

Common schools in America were dominated by Protestant values. In the context of the evolution of American education, this outcome is not hard to understand. The original European immigrants who settled America came to create the perfect religious society in order to escape the religious persecution they felt in Europe. The settlers, led by Jonathan Winthrop and others, were interested in breaking away from the religious persecution they had felt in England in the 1600s when the Catholic Church was in power. After their arrival, schools gradually developed first for the purposes of creating good citizens in the new society who would have the moral upbringing of the Protestant Bible and then later to build a unified nation with a common culture under the teachings of Protestant theology. By the early 1800s and clearly by the end of the 1830s when Irish Catholics were arriving, common public schools had developed in America to establish a unified

country with a common social and political curriculum for all. Schools were run according to the deep-seated Protestant beliefs that had firmly been established in the first 200 years of the country. With the arrival of millions of Irish Catholics and the subsequent desire of Irish Catholics to attend public schools, an obvious conflict arose given the religious beliefs of the Protestants, the religious beliefs of the Catholics, and the common public school curriculum. In particular, funding for the social/political curriculum (which clearly highlighted the Protestant religion) caused a problem in the eyes of Irish Catholics. Significant disagreements occurred over the use of state educational funds used for common public schools.

In the late 1830s and into the 1840s in New York City, where 50% of the residents were foreign-born (Mondale & Patton, 2001, p. 31), Catholics demanded some of the state money that was being used to fund what was called the Public School Society. The Public School Society had evolved from the New York Free School Society, an earlier movement established to ensure public school attendance to create an educated society unified in its support of a common culture. The leading Catholic in New York, Bishop John Hughes, who identified the Irish Catholics as generally poor and desperate for an education, went on to say, "We are unwilling to pay taxes for the purpose of destroying our religion in the minds of our children" (Mondale & Patton, 2001, p. 33). Even before this time, Irish Catholics had begun the usual sequence of events that other oppressed populations had begun in the education of their children. They had begun with home schooling, moved to neighborhood parlor schools, and, eventually, began operating their own schools. All of these were attempts to provide their children with a Catholic upbringing—something as vitally important to Catholics as a Protestant upbringing was to Protestants. Because the common public schools were Protestant-based, Catholics felt forced to educate their children on their own—a typical course for minority populations to take. Virtually all ethnic cultures in America attempted their own schooling measures. Historian Carl Kaestle (1983, p. 166) reported that Catholics were the only group to organize and sustain a sizeable number of schools outside the common public school system. The main objection to the common public school system was the use of the Protestant King James version of the Bible and textbooks, stories, and other teacher materials, as well as the singing of Protestant hymns (Mondale & Patton, 2001, p. 33), which contained anti-Catholic messages. Living as a minority culture within the context of a larger majority culture, the Irish Catholics had to experience the stereotypical thinking of that majority culture. For example, a popular book in its twenty-first edition in 1836 entitled *Practical System of Modern Geography* stated that "The Irish in general are quick of apprehension, active, brave, and hospitable; but are passionate, ignorant, vain, and superstitious" (Kaestle, 1983, p. 88). Public common schools put much emphasis on the assimilation of immigrant children. Assimilation was the intended effect of the common public schools in their primary focus of forming a unified country through a common social and political curriculum. People looked to education as the best way for immigrants to learn Anglo-American Protestant values. Another book of the period stated that Irish immigration would make America the "common sewer of Ireland" (Kaestle, 1983, pp. 161–163). Catholics could hardly send their children to schools which were unabashedly criticizing Irish people and the Catholic religion and overtly attempting to instill dominant culture values into the Irish. The second-generation of Irish declared that "our children become our opponents" as a result of attending common public schools. They saw their parents looked upon as an inferior race and wanted to break away. Schools were teaching children "to feel ashamed of the creed of their forefathers" (Kaestle, 1983, pp. 163–164). Tense feelings permeated society regarding the common public schools and Catholic education.

These tense feelings that had begun as a simmer
in the mid-1820s reached a boiling point by 1838 at
which time Protestants and Catholics were out-
wardly at odds and vehemently arguing about the
nature of the common public schools. In New York,
Governor William Henry Seward was running for election. A major plank in his political platform, one
which he had espoused for a number of years, was
that education was the key to an economically,
politically, and socially strong America. Many others, including Horace Mann, the father of the common public school movement, had been touting
this belief since the signing of the Declaration of
Independence. Seward saw himself as a strong advocate of increased state support for the funding of all
education. He focused on education for a strong
and independent America and realized that if the
Catholics were not getting an education because
they were refusing to attend common public schools,
then other types of education needed to be in place.
Irish Catholics were already being thought of as
lawless paupers, and so the vernacular of the time
reflected Seward's concern (Schuman, 2004, p. 62).
Seward believed in state support for Catholic schools.
He strongly advocated for the education of Catholic
immigrants, particularly the Irish Catholics. At one
point, Seward so harshly attacked the strong anti-Irish
Catholic sentiments that pervaded the society in
the 1830s and 1840s that he denounced the
Americans' hatred of "foreigners" (Spring, 2001a,
p. 88).

Not surprisingly, when the common public
schools remained Protestant-driven into the 1840s,
Irish Catholics simply stopped sending their children
to schools. Governor Seward realized that the anti-
Catholic nature of the common public schools meant
that large portions of American society were being
left uneducated—a threat to American economic
and political strength. He was convinced that Irish
Catholic children would become illiterate juvenile
delinquents who would not only fail to become
contributing members of American society but would

become burdens of it. A Catholic priest in New York named Father Richard Shaw reported that common public schools' anti-Catholic bias had already "created a situation in which some 20,000 children were running the streets of New York without benefit of education because they refused to be a part of a system biased against themselves" (Mondale & Patton, 2001, pp. 33–34). Seward's radical proposal in 1840 was to include Catholic schools as part of the common public school system but to let Catholic schools keep their private charters and religious activities. Historian Vincent Lannie wrote that "Seward urged the establishment of schools that would be acceptable to this minority group and staffed with teachers who spoke the same language and professed the same religious faith as their pupils. Such schools would be administered by Catholic officials but supported with public funds" (Spring, 2001a, p. 88).

As a result of Seward's proposal, the Catholics of New York City petitioned the Board of Alderman for a portion of the money being used to fund common public schools. The general population at first merely scoffed at this petition but later became outraged. The petition in part asked for the restoration of public funds that were discontinued in 1825. Until 1825 Catholic charity schools had received federal aid, but that aid had ended in 1825 (Kaestle, 1983, p. 168). Catholic thinking was that the precedence of previous federal aid and its subsequent removal would justify a granting of renewed aid from the local level. In their petition, the Catholics itemized their complaints regarding the Protestant domination of common public schools. The petition specifically addressed the following complaints:

1. Religious instruction including reading and study of the (Protestant) Bible was sectarian and broke the supposition of non-sectarian schools.
2. Elementary reading lessons were built around Protestant writers who were clearly against Catholicism. For example, the word *popery,* an insult to the Catholic religion, was repeatedly found in readings.

3. In spite of the efforts of some Protestants to eliminate the anti-Catholic curriculum, it was impossible for them to do so because Protestants could not always recognize the anti-Catholic curriculum. (Principals in New York had been ordered to go through their textbooks by hand to painstakingly eliminate anti-Catholic passages.)

4. The anti-Catholic public schools forced Catholics to open their own schools. This caused double-taxation. (Kaestle, 1983, p. 169, reports that the precedence of parental responsibility in education was a common Catholic argument against taxation for common public schools.)

5. Catholics believed that public schools should not support religion and were willing to remove all religion from public schools during school hours. They went so far as to support a non-religious watchdog to insure this removal of religion (Spring, 2001a, p. 88).

Not surprisingly, Seward's proposal and the Catholics' petition created huge controversy and anger and, if it was possible, split Protestants and Catholics even more. As scoff turned into outrage, the Board of Aldermen of New York City and the New York City Common Council held meetings to discuss the proposal and the petition. Meanwhile, Protestants were consolidating against any change in the common public school system. They declared that if Catholics were willing to postpone religious instruction until after school hours, they should be willing to instruct the children attending Public School Society schools after school hours (Spring, 2001a, p. 89).

Arguments and discussions continued. By 1842 the disagreements became so heated that riots broke out between anti-Catholics and the Irish Catholics. Catholics were attacked and beaten on the streets, in their homes, and wherever they hid. Even the home of Bishop John Hughes, located behind the landmark St. Patrick's Cathedral, was attacked. Bishop Hughes was intensely involved in the issue, had partnered with Seward on both the proposal and the petition, and had earlier gone on record to say that, "The public schools taught children that Catholics were necessarily, morally, intellectually, infallibly, a stupid race" (Kaestle, 1983, p. 168). In 1843 in Philadelphia things got even worse. After some Catholic leaders agreed that schools could be changed rather than maintaining separate Catholic schools, feelings even among Catholics intensified. Concessions and compromises were discussed regarding Bible use and religious instruction. The Philadelphia Public School Board ruled that Catholics could read their own verses of the Catholic Douay Bible in common public schools and could be excused from other religious instruction. Catholics were satisfied with the ruling, but Protestants were livid. They viewed the decision as a ploy by the Catholics to rid the schools of the Protestant Bible. The upheaval over versions of the Bible resulted in the Philadelphia Bible Riots of 1843 in which thirteen people died and churches were burned to the ground. Those accused of these crimes and brought to trial were not punished. In other parts of the country further conflict between Catholics and anti-Catholics over schooling led to more riots and demonstrations.

By the late 1840s, the Catholics were beginning to realize the strength of the Protestants' resolve to maintain common public schools as a bastion of Protestantism with an anti-Catholic backlash. They were beginning to see that they were not going to succeed at winning the points they were after as delineated in the petition to the New York City Board of Alderman. They were also observing that the establishment of individual Catholic schools was moving slowly. Realizing all of this, the Catholics set up a series of council meetings at which their leaders would begin to discuss the planning of their own system of education. These meetings, called Plenary Councils, had as their primary focus and major theme that Catholic religion should not be separated from other instruction.

Breaking Away

In the end, Catholics realized that they had been put into a position of having to establish their own system of schools to save their children from a Protestant education and to raise their children in the Catholic tradition. The Plenary Councils of 1852, 1866, and 1884, all held in Baltimore, accomplished this goal. At the First Plenary Council parents were told by church leaders that they had a responsibility to "watch over the purity of their [children's] faith and morals with jealous vigilance." Catholic parents were urged to give their children a Christian education "based on religious principles accompanied by religious practices and always subordinate to religious influence." The council urged that all possible sacrifices be made for the establishment of Catholic schools (Spring, 2001a, p. 91).

When the Second Plenary Council met in 1866, its major goal was to emphasize "that religious teaching and religious training should form part of every system of school education." This council also expressed concern regarding the large number of delinquent Catholic youths who were being sent to Protestant reformatories. The council recommended the establishment of Catholic industrial schools to care for delinquent Catholic youths (Spring, 2001a, p. 91).

The Third Plenary Council, in 1884, sent forth decrees for the establishment of a system of Catholic schools. The council warned that the continued trend toward secular education could undermine Christianity and argued that all religious groups were calling for a Christian education in schools, reflecting a common concern for the preservation of religious faith. The council considered the creation of Catholic schools as beneficial to the state because such schools would create better citizens by educating better Christians (Spring, 2001a, p. 91).

To achieve the objectives of ensuring a Catholic education, the council decreed that every church establish a parish school and that all Catholic parents send their children to Catholic schools. The fol-

lowing decrees of the Third Plenary Council articulated the ideals of Catholic education in the United States:

> I. That near every church a parish school, where one does not yet exist, is to be built and maintained in perpetuum within two years of the promulgation of this council, unless the bishop should decide that becauseof serious difficulties a delay may be granted . . .
>
> IV. That all Catholic parents are bound to send their children to the parish school, unless it is evident that a sufficient training in religion is given either in their own homes, or in other Catholic schools; or when because of sufficient reason, approved by the Bishop, with all due precautions and safeguards, it is licit to send them to other schools. What constitutes a Catholic school is left to the decision of the Bishop (Spring, 2001a, p. 91).

The Plenary Councils and their decrees symbolized the end of the argument between Catholics and Protestants regarding common public education and education in general. The beginnings of a school system separate from the common public schools and, specifically, for the education of Catholic children in a Catholic tradition solidified the idea that American education would be more than a single system of schools. As the Catholics came to call the common public schools "Protestant Schools," Protestants came to call parochial schools Catholic schools. This two-tiered system of common and parochial schools meant that Horace Mann's idea of a common public school for all did not and would not work in America.

Post 1884: A Continuance of Anti-Catholic Sentiment

After the Plenary Councils were completed and Catholic parochial schools were established, the anti-Irish Catholic sentiment continued. This anti-Catholic sentiment could not only be observed in countless pulpit sermons around the nation's non-Catholic churches, but at community gatherings, both

private and public. An example of the pervasiveness of this sentiment in society is the wide popularity of Reverend Richard Harcourt's book *Conspiracy: The American Public Schools,* published in 1890. The purpose of this book was not only to criticize Catholicism in general but to continue the attack on Catholic views of education by ridiculing the newly forming parochial schools post-Plenary Councils. Harcourt made fun of the use of the rosary for praying and other traditions sacred to Catholics. The noted and well-known political cartoonist Thomas Nast illustrated the book with discriminating caricatures made to belittle Catholics and Catholic ideas. One illustration depicted Irish people as apes and predicted Irish apes would run the country in the year 2000 (Reese, 2005, pp. 53–56).

After losing the battle with Protestants to change common public schools to accommodate their religion and culture, Catholics separated themselves from common public schools, which they called Protestant Schools, and established Catholic parochial schools. This separation of education did not lessen the discrimination and prejudice put upon Irish Catholics by America's dominant culture through the 1890s and beyond.

End of the Era

Near the end of this era of American education, the 1880s play movement called for adult-directed play (as opposed to free play) in order to promote cooperative, good citizens. The idea was to socialize children to the American way by controlling play. Playgrounds, sandlots, parks, clubs, summer school, public baths, school nurses, school lunch, and neighborhood schools were some of the important programs that developed at the time. They easily fit into the Lockean philosophy of writing on blank slates. Most of these activities were identified as 100% Americanization programs. In 1871 William T. Harris, appointed the U.S. Commissioner of Education, reflected the same idea when he stated that the first requirement of school was order: **Conformity was**

Conformity, the first rule of order

A concept attributed in 1871 to United States Commissioner of Education William T. Harris, who had proclaimed that the first requirement of school was order

his first rule of order (Spring, 2001, pp. 149–150). Playgrounds were attached to schools to offer after-school activities to prevent crime. Healthy living was provided by the rest of the above-listed play movement innovations. These different dynamics extended the social roles of schools. America was creating school reform movements to address the same issues that had concerned the Massachusetts Bay Colony.

During Reconstruction after the Civil War schooling took on a new role—to provide workers for the new industrial society. The **manual training movement** created by Calvin Woodard at Washington University in St. Louis established courses in such subjects as woodworking, drafting, and metalworking. Woodward believed that a liberal education included working with one's hands and that all children should be taught a liberal education through courses like these (Webb, 2006, p. 179). Though these concepts were debated in his time and remain controversial today, Woodward's ideas evolved into vocational education to train students to work in the American economy. This idea flourished as vocational guidance became the process of matching students to available jobs. The early junior high schools added to the popularity of the comprehensive high schools by providing vocational education through vocational guidance. The most important piece of legislation connected with the development of vocational education and the **comprehensive school movement** in this era was the Smith-Hughes Act of 1917, which would be passed in the next era. This act detailed education for specific job occupations and federally funded programs to support those curricula. The most important school factor linked to the development of vocational education would be the differentiated curriculum of the next era.

Manual training movement

Refers to education with the use of hands such as metalwork, woodwork, or drafting; considered the beginning of the vocational education movement

Comprehensive school movement

Developed during the industrial revolution featuring differentiated instruction, vocational education, and vocational guidance

Glossary

100% Americanization—This term describes the plethora of programs and activities meant to promote the values of the dom-

inant culture in both schools and society beginning in the nineteenth century.

Blank Slate—The part of Lockean philosophy that refers to humans being born without knowledge and thus having blank slates and making it necessary for schools to shape learning.

Calvinism—A philosophy associated with the Protestant theology of the Puritans that believed humans were born in sin and needed the sin to be driven out.

Cato's Letters—A series of anonymously published letters from 1720 to 1723 declaring the desire for increased individual rights in the colonies.

Common School Movement—The school model popular in the nineteenth century that attempted to bring all White children to a common school with a common curriculum based on the social and political primary factors in order to ideologically manage a dominant culture based society.

Comprehensive School Movement—A school movement developed during the industrial revolution that featured differentiated instruction, vocational education, and vocational guidance.

Conformity, the First Rule of Order—A concept attributed in 1871 to United States Commissioner of Education William T. Harris, who had proclaimed that the first requirement of school was order.

Deculturalization—The stripping away of others' culture by depriving them of their language, customs, traditions, celebrations, religion, and education.

Instruments of Religion—This term has been used to describe schools as vehicles for teaching religious indoctrination.

Manual Training Movement—Established by Calvin Woodward as a liberal education, this term referred to education with the use of hands such as metalworking, woodworking, and drafting and served as the beginning of the much larger vocational education movement.

Massachusetts Bay Colony—The early American settlement established in the seventeenth century by Puritans seeking religious freedom and economic independence.

Massachusetts Law of 1642 and the Old Deluder Satan Law—Considered the first two major laws in the evolution of American educational history.

McGuffey's Readers—A school text created for the common school movement devised to promote national unity.

Monitorial System—A system of school management and

instruction that incorporated the use of student helpers (monitors) in the delivery of lessons.

National Unity—The push by American schools in the nineteenth century to be independent of the influence of other nations and to establish a pride in national spirit.

New England Primer—The major textbook for American schools in the eighteenth and early nineteenth centuries featuring Americanized spelling, grammar, and reading.

Ornamental Knowledge—Information taught in school curricula of the seventeenth and eighteenth centuries not directly related to occupational skills; for example, etiquette, debate, or how to be a gentleman.

Patriotic Americans—An eighteenth- and nineteenth-century term meant to create a citizenry that was separate and distinct from European influence.

Plenary Councils—A sequence of three nineteenth-century meetings held by Irish Catholic leaders to devise a plan for the education of Irish Catholics resulting in the beginning of a parochial school system of education.

Republican Motherhood—The idea that sought the expansion of mothers' traditional role beyond that within the family to that of women becoming mothers of a growing nation.

Schools as Instruments of Government Policy—During the common school movement, school curricula centered on political and social primary factors, and thus, schools went away from being instruments of religion and toward being instruments of the national government.

Unified National Spirit—A term meant to create a patriotic American national unity by establishing school curricula based only on American songs, celebrations, holidays, literature, and so on.

Utilitarian Knowledge—Information taught in school curricula of the eighteenth and nineteenth centuries directly related to occupational skills, for example, blacksmithing, carpentry, accounting, and so on.

Webster's American Dictionary of the English Language—A major source for the Americanization of the English language in the nineteenth century.

Review

1. From where did America get its form of education?
2. What overriding philosophy of living and learning was the norm in the 1600s?

3. What theology was dominant?
4. Describe the first two laws created for American education.
5. Describe the three general types of schools that were developed during this era.
6. Explain republicanism.
7. It is 1650 in a small town near Boston. Create a school day's events for a ten-year-old.
8. What dramatic educational change took place between 1720 and 1723?
9. What set of publications helped create the change (above)?
10. Name three national leaders at this time and explain their beliefs.
11. Describe the dominant culture.
12. Explain how republicanism moved into nationalism.
13. It is 1782 in Philadelphia. You are a national leader who has been asked to create a charter for education in America. What would you include in your charter?
14. Summarize Horace Mann's ideas regarding education at this time.
15. Describe the common school movement.
16. Explain the educational ideas of Froebel, Pestalozzi, Lancaster, and Rousseau.
17. Explain the specific situation at this time with each of the following groups: Native Americans, Asian Americans, Mexican Americans, African Americans, women, Irish Catholics.
18. Describe some of the play movement ideas.
19. It is 1848 and you are a woman who wants to be a teacher. What will you do?
20. What thoughts do you have regarding the history of American education?

Selected Topics for Further Study

1. Puritans
2. Protestants
3. Massachusetts Bay Colony
4. Schools in America prior to 1720
5. Calvinisn
6. Cato's Letters
7. Thomas Jefferson
8. Noah Webster
9. Ben Franklin
10. The United States Constitution
11. The Bible

12. The Gold Rush of 1849
13. The Transcontinental Railroad
14. The common school
15. Reconstruction
16. The Emancipation Proclamation
17. Population demographics in America from 1600 to 1830
18. Irish Catholics
19. Native American culture
20. Mexican American culture

The Industrial Revolution

Good Times Roll Into Bad

Industrialization

The transition from an agricultural to an industrial society

Urbanization

Increase in the number of persons living in cities as a result of industrialization and immigration in the nineteenth century

Three main social, economic, and political factors strongly affected schooling in this era. Since Reconstruction, America had been moving from an agrarian to an industrial society. **Industrialization** led to increased **urbanization**. Larger numbers of people moved to cities to find work in the factories. In 1920, for the first time in history, more people were living in cities and towns than in rural areas. Factories and businesses were starting to dominate the economy. Urban school facilities were stretched as attendance soared. While industrialization and urbanization increased, new waves of immigrants were arriving from Southern and Eastern Europe to put even more demands on cities and on schools. From 1900 to 1920, 900,000 immigrants arrived per year (Webb, 2006, pp. 214–220).

The American educational system was taking on broader social and economic functions. The play movement changed schools forever by adding health programs as well as after-school school and commu-

nity activities. Of special importance to the future of American education was the decision to organize the school system to improve human capital as a means of economic growth. This new organization resulted in the comprehensive school and its emphasis on vocational education, vocational guidance, the junior high school, and the science of educational measurement. Politically, the reorganization created ideological management struggles over how to make schools best conform to the industrial model of education.

Leading Ideological Managers of This Era

Scientific method
A system of measuring time management and cost-effectiveness to arrive at standard operations for efficiency

Taylorism
Scientific methods applied to factories and schools

Frederick W. Taylor became well-known for his **scientific method** of organizing factories. His idea to create standardization for cost-effectiveness in factories was adopted by schools and identified as the factory model. In this model, work is standardized so that everyone has a compartment and within that compartment everything is done in a standardized fashion. This standardized cost efficiency moved education out of the common school movement into what could be called the comprehensive school movement. The basic principles of **Taylorism** included hierarchal control, social efficiency thinking (training workers for their best job and making them cooperate), and scientific management for environmental control. Standardization for cost-effectiveness included planning, record keeping, directions, instructions, procedures, schedules, and lines of control. The chief component of the comprehensive school movement was the differentiated curriculum. With sorting and training students as its purpose, the differentiated curriculum attempted to classify students into educational tracks that led to specialized jobs. The most common educational tracks were vocational, college-bound, and general. In addition, many high schools added the business track. Established for the purpose of training students as human capital in the Industrial Revolution, the differentiated curriculum's goal was to create an organized workforce to establish the United States as a world economic power. The fallout from this goal was the escalation of social classification and discrimination caused by sorting and training placement techniques which reflected dominant culture values and favoritism. As part of the 100% Americanization programs, clubs, student government, assemblies, organized sports, and social events flourished. By 1890, school attendance had risen to 203,000 children. By 1900, this figure rose to 519,000 and by 1912, 1.1 million children were attending school (Spring, 2001a, p. 255).

The most popular African American leader in America at this time was still Booker T. Washington. He delivered a speech in 1895, later to be called the **Atlanta or Southern Compromise**, which seemed to mollify White industrialists by suggesting that African Americans would be satisfied with segregated education in industrial schools, in order to become the backbone of the workforce for American factories, without pushing for civil rights. In spite of rousing disagreement and debate by W. E. B. Du Bois and others, Washington's ideas prevailed. In this same year, *Plessy v. Ferguson* was passed. Combined with Washington's leadership, this famous court case that declared "separate" to be "equal" kept the focus on segregated education for at least the next 60 years until *Brown v. Board of Education of Topeka* was passed. Segregated schools for Asian and Mexican Americans continued while Native Americans found themselves in White-run boarding schools. New immigrants were beginning to understand the dominant culture plan as 100% Americanization programs proliferated in the comprehensive school.

John Dewey saw **schools as social centers** where life and the work world could be combined. Auditoriums were built to provide easy access to the public. Lyceums put on by various groups promoted the American flag, patriotism, and the **assimilation** of minorities into the dominant culture. Student government, school newspapers, and a variety of student clubs to promote democracy flourished. Junior high schools were built to facilitate voca-

Atlanta (Southern) Compromise
Said to be the result of a speech by Booker T. Washington promoting industrial education for African Americans

Schools as social centers
John Dewey's idea in the early twentieth century to connect the school and the workplace with schools as the hub of the community

Assimilation
The process of taking on the values and lifestyles of the dominant culture by dominated or minority cultures

tional education within the comprehensive school model. Coinciding with the rise of vocational education, vocational guidance programs proliferated to reduce inefficiency in the distribution of human resources. Aptitude tests and career interest tests became standards in the comprehensive school model. Dewey's influence was most apparent in his leadership in Progressive Education which linked to the general **Progressive Reform Movement**, which began in the late nineteenth century but rose to prominence at the turn of the twentieth century. The remarkable demographic and industrial changes taking place in America fostered a Progressive Movement to address issues such as:

- Regulating the labor of women and children
- Improving working conditions
- Combating unfair business practices
- Overturning corruption in politics
- Making government more democratic and more responsive to the people
- Improving conditions in the urban slums

The **efficiency movement** that resulted from these efforts created new focus on the efficiency of school operations, differentiated curriculum, support for child study, and measurement techniques. The Progressive Movement's ideas directly related to schooling were the following:

- Making schools more sanitary
- Getting schools to have more sunlight and open air
- Making schools more conducive to creative activity
- Lowering teacher/pupil ratios
- Adding basic health care and food services
- Establishing night schools for adults and immigrants
- Committing to schools as social centers
- Committing to administrative and pedagogical changes
- Using the Taylor model of standardization

Progressive Reform Movement

A movement in the late nineteenth and early twentieth century that addressed issues such as labor regulations, corruption in politics, education

Efficiency movement

The successor of the progressive movement, this movement used scientific methods to make schools operationally and instructionally efficient

- Using experts for scientific measurement of students and the business of schools (Dewey, 1938/1997)

One form of scientific management was the measurement of students' intelligence. Alfred Binet, Lewis M. Terman, and Herbert Goddard along with Edward L. Thorndike developed mental capacity tests, which later evolved into IQ tests. Binet developed the tests to measure mental retardation while Terman developed the Stanford/Binet Intelligence test to determine students' IQ. Terman argued that his test supported the nature versus nurture argument and suggested that schools could still be good for non-academic goals. Goddard, who helped develop the Alpha Beta Army Intelligence tests, saw a societal problem in the fact that more and more people were moving from the country to the cities. He claimed that these people were of low intelligence and that crime would result. He believed the top 4% of intelligence of the population should rule (Spring, 2001a, p. 299). Calling this the aristocracy of intelligence for democracy, he thought it represented the perfect government. Thorndike, who taught the first course and wrote the first textbook on scientific management, became the scientific expert on test construction. He thought tests should be long and hard to develop the ability to stick to a task. By the 1920s, Carl Brigham had developed the SATs or Scholastic Aptitude Tests. These leaders in scientific measurement were all members of the mainstream dominant culture. Among them, both John Dewey and William C. Bagley criticized the standardized tests as being stereotypical and labeling (Webb, 2006, p. 229). They believed that mental measurement tests created by dominant culture scientists discriminated against dominated cultures by reflecting only the context of the dominant culture. Indeed, Terman, Thorndike, and Goddard espoused improving the population via sterilization, restrictive immigration, and selective breeding based on the results of these tests (Spring, 2001a, p. 302). Their work led to, among many

other developments, the 1924 Immigration Act, which blatantly restricted non-Whites from immigrating based on information from IQ tests. As smaller school boards were established, power and duties increased for school administrators who relished the opportunities and viewed themselves as educational experts. These school administrators, unwavering in their support for standardized and IQ tests, thus supported and promoted them within the 100% Americanization programs.

As the era came to a close, the industrial society was solidly established, schools under the differentiated curriculum were fostering a workforce to be used as human capital in the rush to establish the United States as a world economic power, and 100% Americanization programs were escalating the use of schools as purveyors of government policy. Segregated schools were the norm for minority populations which remained dominated cultures.

Good Times Roll Into Bad:
The 1920s, the 1930s, and the 1940s

Social, political, and economic factors created the ideologies dominating this era. As a result, the comprehensive school movement realized its full force as a factory model of vocationally oriented schooling sorting and training students to generate human capital to establish America as a global economic power. At the same time, the comprehensive school movement increased its 100% Americanization programs which put national unity via its dominant culture at the top of everyone's school agenda. Epitomized by the creation of such agencies as the American Legion, this agenda promoted the growth of schools as social centers so that they could shape society to control all "anti-American tendencies." Playgrounds, sandlots, auditoriums, organized sports, school assemblies, student senates, and school newspapers were some of the major arenas more fully developed by schools to indoctrinate students in 100% Americanization. "Social efficiency" became a catch phrase to hitch on to the previous

Lancasterian model of "no idle moments" and Taylor's standardization for production ideas.

John Dewey and his followers, however, argued that education should be a process of living in and of itself, not a preparation for future living. Dewey wanted much more than only vocational education. His ideas for a full experience at school led to strong support for such ideas as assemblies, lyceums, and student associations. The school as a social center attempted to combine life and work (Dewey, 1938/1997). Social efficiency theory carried on through the popularity of the object lesson plan and a plethora of pedagogical attempts to capture student interests (Webb, 2006, p. 153). The comprehensive school as a factory model identified students as its products, and the Gary Plan for work/study became popular in hundreds of schools. Although new freedoms for women were on the horizon, rigid rules for teachers remained and affected women, who continued to dominate the teaching ranks.

The Economy and the Education of Youths

The economy was headed for disaster, but before the crash and the Great Depression the 1920s played out as a period of economic prosperity. Employment stabilized, automobile production proliferated, and many new millionaires were created as a result of the Industrial Revolution. In addition, the Nineteenth Amendment, giving women voting rights, was passed by Congress in 1919 and ratified in 1920. This new freedom spurred women to a new sense of liberation resulting in many lifestyle changes. Also, Prohibition was passed in 1917 and ratified in 1919 via the Eighteenth Amendment, leading to the proliferation of speakeasies, rum-running, organized crime, and an increase in the consumption of alcohol. While women received more freedoms and alcohol was becoming more popular, the Jazz Age brought flappers and a rage for modern dance and art. Whites began appreciating African American music, automobiles increased mobility and freedom, and the good times rolled. The freedoms and excesses of this era

came to an abrupt end with the stock market crash of 1929 and the ensuing economic Depression.

The crisis of the Depression brought about a new emphasis on the education of youths. George Counts, in a speech entitled *Dare Progressive Education Be Progressive?* (Counts, 1932) called for teachers to reconstruct society (Webb, 2006, p. 254). The speech was the birth of the idea of **social reconstruction**. The supposition was that capitalism failed to fully use science and technology for the benefit of human capital. The idea was to forge a new spirit of healthy and cooperative good living. New knowledge would free people from poverty, and teachers should teach the new knowledge because their first allegiance was to children, not private economic interests. Thus, teachers would be the social reconstructionists. With unions gaining strength, the National Education Association (NEA) adopted this idea and reached for power. This joining of forces resulted in what is described by Counts as the **social efficiency doctrine**. This doctrine claimed that the future social needs of children were found in the teaching of cooperation within the differentiated curriculum. These ideas along with the economic crises began the further divided alliances among local school administrators, boards of education, and local elites over school spending.

By 1932, schools were in serious economic trouble. By 1934 school enrollment was up 750,000 since 1930, and revenues were down $278 million. Nearly 20,000 schools were closed, leaving a million children with no school to attend. Some schools were operating only three to six months per year. Because students in some schools were required to pay tuition and/or bring in their own supplies, poverty prevented some 3.5 million children from attending. Of all schoolteachers, 80% were female until schools began policies to keep married women out of teaching because they were taking jobs from men. In addition, some schools found ways to eliminate senior teachers, both women and men, so that new teachers could be hired at lower salaries. Money

Social reconstruction

This concept, suggested by George Counts in 1932, promoted schools as the institutions for reconstructing a healthy economic society

Social efficiency doctrine

This doctrine promotes the teaching of cooperation within the differentiated curriculum to accommodate social needs to students for salaries was so tight that teachers were often paid in vegetables, and the eigtheenth-century phenomenon of "boarding 'round" (teachers living with their students) became popular again (Webb, 2006, pp. 245–246).

In 1933, with the creation of the New Deal, the federal government became actively involved in education and never looked back. The government began creating programs for a renewed economy and included schools as a main factor in the process. Programs such as the National Youth Administration, the Civilian Conservation Corps, the Public Works Administration, and the Works Progress Administration had school components that included classroom instruction in conservation followed by physical labor. The physical labor included building libraries, classrooms, and schools. The largest of the New Deal programs, the Works Progress Administration, fostered the hiring of 100,000 teachers for adult education, preschool literacy, nutrition, and school building repair (Webb, 2006, pp. 249–253).

By the end of the 1930s, comprehensive schools were in full force featuring 100% Americanization programs, differentiated curriculum, increased testing, and an emphasis in vocational education for the purposes of developing human capital. Urban education attendance had skyrocketed, and as a result, the general curriculum ballooned in size as lower income and minority students were tracked into it. New government programs such as the Federal Deposit Insurance Corporation and Social Security were established to prevent another Depression. The first Red Scare (fear of Communism) following the end of World War I was to some degree reduced by the attention to more demanding economic problems.

In 1924, the Indian Citizenship Act was passed granting the right of citizenship to Native Americans. In 1928 the Bureau of Indian Affairs (BIA) generated the Merriam Report calling for the end of boarding schools, the reversal of the assimilation policy, and a renewed focus on Native American culture. The

report led to the Indian Reorganization Act of 1934, which provided federal funding for self-governance, and the John O'Malley Act of 1934, which required federal funding of Native American lunch and transportation programs. Another major attempt for African American education that included both the South and the North took place between 1910 and 1930 and resulted in increased numbers of segregated common schools for Blacks. Though literacy rates were climbing, segregated schools led to economic exploitation of Blacks because these schools were inferior, employed inferior teachers, and provided a curriculum promoting habits and values for menial labor. The entire focus of segregated schools was to reinforce a belief in White superiority.

By this time, however, groups such as the **National Association for the Advancement of Colored People** (NAACP) in 1908 and in 1929 the **League of United Latin American Citizens** (LULAC) were formed to lead renewed efforts to end deculturalization and foster equality. These organizations began pursuing with some success the rights of the dominated cultures. LULAC, for example, pursued court cases throughout the 1930s which demanded scientific proof of segregation's effectiveness.

Media and Moral Dilemma

This era added another dimension to the moral development of American children. As the film industry developed, many educators and other social commentators voiced a concern that movies would detract from the moral and political Americanization of America's youths. Many feared that freedom of expression in the movie industry might break down moral and patriotic order. This fear led to a national discussion and debate over **censorship**. The question was whether to have government censorship or to allow self-censorship. Seeing their power threatened by those favoring government censorship, the Motion Pictures Producers and Distributors of America (MPPDA) wooed the NEA to gain support for self-censorship. This partnership resulted in many pro-

National Association for the Advancement of Colored People

This association was established early in the twentieth century to identify and promote issues of concern to African Americans

League of United Latin American Citizens

This organization was established in the twentieth century to identify and promote issues affecting U.S. citizens of Latin American origin or descent

Censorship

The debate over whether the movie industry or the federal government should censor television and movies to ensure the proper development of children.

self-censorship speeches and industry-driven movie appreciation courses. However, educators thought that movies, and later radio, television, and even commercial literature, were stealing the minds of children from teachers. Joy Elmer Morgan of the NEA added the idea that advertisers were taking the place of mothers, fathers, teachers, pastors, and priests in forming children's attitudes. Morgan also thought that advertisers were exploiting children as consumers. The famous Payne Studies, which determined that movies could have a detrimental effect on children, resulted from the discussion. Movie appreciation courses proliferated, and movie guides for teachers were produced so that movies and schools could work together to control students' minds (Spring, 2001a, pp. 346–354).

Similar debates regarding moral and political development of students were seen in the radio and comic book industries. With the involvement of the Federal Communications Commission (FCC) and production codes, guidelines for children's radio shows and comic books tempered the radio and comic book industries and, later, the television industry so that moral and political hopes for children would not be dashed. Though the industries initially won the battle for ideological management regarding censorship, they were later joined by the FCC and other agencies in preparing guidelines for media control.

The Birth of the National Association of Colored Women's Clubs

By the nineteenth century women's roles in American society had been quite clearly established. They were subordinate. Based in part on the religious upbringings of the nation, women found their place beneath men regarding personal/social class status and indeed in nearly every identifiable category. They could not enter the professions; they could not own a business; they could not vote in elections; they could not keep accounts; they could not go places and do things that men did; they could not express

ideas or opinions outside of the home. In short, they had no voice. Their place within the family itself was indicative of their place within society. If there was a place for the voice of women, surely it was in the home. Seventeenth-century early Americans had already determined that women were natural nurturers and teachers, morally more uplifting than men and, thus, better equipped to do the child rearing. However, according to a study conducted regarding the role of the colonial family (Demos, 1970, pp. 183–186), women were found to be subordinate to men based on the premise, "He for God only, she for God in him." Historian Joel Spring (2001a, p. 28) interprets this to mean that women were to bow to the God in men, and men were to assume the spiritual care of women. In legal matters, the married woman was at the mercy of her husband; she was without rights to own property, make contracts, or sue for damages. Surely, this subordinate status put women in a position of unequal footing with regard to nearly every facet of life, including personal/social status, with the exception of child rearing, which men clearly called upon women to undertake and within which, by and large, they excelled.

If the above describes the conditions for White women in American society in the nineteenth century, imagine what conditions were like for African American women, who were clearly looked upon as beneath the status of both White men and White women. The combined issues of gender role and race role perceived by American society of the 1800s were such that African American women were relegated to the lowest position. Their rights, privileges, and opportunities were limited to an even further degree than those of White women simply because of their skin color. As if this was not enough, the one bastion of civility for White women, leadership role in family child rearing, was affected for African American women by dominant culture attitudes as well. Although African American women excelled at child rearing as did White women, their opportunity to do so was much more difficult. Indeed, the nature and disorganization of slave families were a breeding ground for dysfunction because family members were sold at the discretion of the slave owner, marriages dissolved, and fathers disappeared because they were sold or killed, or perhaps just ran away.

This subordinate status of women, both White and Black, led necessarily to increased efforts on the parts of courageous and dedicated leaders to obtain an equal ground for women in American status. Though their paths are interwoven and finally joined, White women and Black women weave their way toward equal rights from different perspectives and on different plains. Certain people, events, and groups have contributed immensely to the progress that has been made by both groups since the beginning of the nineteenth century. Surely, the birth of the National Association of Colored Women's Clubs (NACWC) has not been the total picture of status reform for American women, particularly African American women; however, the NACWC plays a significant and symbolic role in the development of women's, and thus humans' rights in America since the 1800s. The work of the NACWC and the organizations it grew out of and spawned provides a picture of the issues that were addressed on the way to increased status for women, in particular, African American women.

The Women's Rights Movement began in 1848 in Seneca Falls, New York. It was there that a convention of men and women was held to discuss the rights of women. In fact, some of the earliest leaders in the women's movement attended the convention. Sojourner Truth, Elizabeth Cady Stanton, William Wells Brown, Charles Lenox Remond, and Frederick Douglass all attended and took leadership roles at this convention. Douglass had previously written in his publication *North Star* that "Right is of no sex" (Wesely, 1984, p. 2). The right being discussed at this convention was the right to vote. It was Elizabeth Cady Stanton who made the motion that, "It is the duty of women in this country to secure themselves their sacred right to the election franchise"

(Wesely, 1984, p. 2). Notably, the motion was seconded by Frederick Douglass, who would go on to become an icon of the movement and a revered figure in the NACWC. Stanton and other members of this first convention, Lucretia Mott and Susan B. Anthony, were leaders in the formation of the National Women's Suffrage Association (NWSA) in 1851. They had organized conferences and conventions throughout the 1840s that dealt with a multiplicity of women's issues but mostly voting rights. By 1866, NWSA changed its name to the Equal Rights Association in order to identify its main ambition more clearly. The objective of the group remained that of universal suffrage. These early examples of organizations are indicators of the beginning of efforts toward women's rights. However, even before the 1840s, there were significant numbers of societies and clubs formed on local levels by African American women. Most of these were anti-slavery and literary societies that brought local women together to address local concerns. On December 4, 1833, for example, the American Anti-Slavery Society was formed. The importance of this group was in its encouragement of women into its membership (Black and White) and the work it did to establish schools, campaign against the Fugitive Slave Laws, and to assist in the Underground Railroad. The agendas of these groups included a heavy emphasis on moral and religious issues to guide people to live their lives honestly and in a wholesome fashion. The importance of morality and religion was interwoven with the importance of education, especially literacy. Education was encouraged most strongly for children, but it was encouraged also for adults.

Typically, societies, or clubs, were located in the northern so-called free states. White women who joined the anti-slavery cause were Lucretia Mott, Abby Kelly Foster, Lucy Stone, and Susan B. Anthony. One African American spokesperson of the time, author Fannie Barrier Williams, declared that "Among colored women, the club is the effort of the few competent on the behalf of the many incompetent" (Wesely, 1984, p. 2). Her statement is historically accurate as a cadre of well-identified, competent women assumed leadership positions and attempted to uplift others while they climbed into better positions themselves. This early observation connects clearly with African American women escalating the importance of the African American traditional values of education by attending colleges in higher numbers throughout the mid-1800s. In fact, most of the NACWC's key leaders were college graduates. Other Black women who led the anti-slavery cause were Francis Ellen, Watkins Harper, Sojourner Truth, Harriet Tubman, and Amanda Smith. These early church clubs became the models for the proliferation of later local club work, which by the end of the century would gain great speed and produce great numbers of clubs both locally and statewide with thousands of members.

In New York City in the 1860s a women's club was formed to investigate ways to further the causes of women. This club of White women was called the Sorosis Club. For its twenty-first anniversary celebration, this club sent out a call to approximately 100 other women's clubs inviting them to send delegates to its convention in New York City. On March 20, 1889, 61 clubs represented by over 100 delegates met to form the Federation of Women's Clubs (FWC). A constitution was adopted the next year and conventions were begun on a biennial basis beginning in 1892. The FWC became the first national organization of women's clubs. Though its constitution, written in 1890, did not allow the admittance of African Americans, not much was made of it until 1899. In spite of this drawback, the FWC became a subtle motivating factor for the eventual organization of the NACWC. Other events had been and were occurring to advance Black women's causes. Throughout the 1860s, 1870s, and 1880s, higher education institutions such as Oberlin College, Fisk University, Wilberforce College, Wellesley College, Vassar, Cornell, Howard University, Atlanta University, Chicago University, and others had not only been

admitting Black women, but they were also graduating them. In 1862 Mary Jane Patterson became the first Black woman to graduate from Oberlin College. Mary Church Terrell, Anna Julia Cooper, and Ida Gibbs graduated in 1884. Spelman College for Black women opened in 1881. These colleges and their graduates opened the doors to many professions for women who from this time on began joining the ranks of nurses, physicians, lawyers, teachers, musicians, authors, editors, columnists, and businesswomen. The women who served as these examples also provided motivation for the organizations of hundreds of Black women's clubs on local levels and then state levels to consider community and state issues and to advance the establishment of education systems for the purposes of uplifting the oppressed masses. In addition to these goals and their desire to be morally uplifting, the clubs emphasized equality of opportunity with men and suffrage. While there were White women's clubs which were willing and able to work with Black women's clubs to gain equality together, the most common occurrence was the increased formation of separate Black women's clubs in local communities, which would over time evolve into state organizations and which would eventually develop the National Association of Colored Women's Clubs. For all practical purposes, though there were multiple exceptions on both sides, White women's clubs and Black women's clubs were developing separately. By the 1890s, local clubs and state organizations were headed toward national affiliation in both groups.

Among the many, some of the early leaders in organizing Black women's clubs on local and state levels included Josephine St. Pierre Ruffin, Hallie Quinn Brown, Mary Church Terrell, Victoria Earle Mathews, Josephine Silone Yates, Fannie Jackson Coppin, Margaret Murray Washington, and Agnes Jones Adams.

Josephine St. Pierre Ruffin was a charter member of the Massachusetts School Suffrage Association and worked diligently with Lucy Stone and Julia

Ward Howe on issues of universal suffrage. She was a member of ten state women's clubs and an officer in most. These clubs were active in women's rights issues, and they led Ruffin to establish a major national contributor to Black women's clubs, the Women's New Era Club, founded in 1893. With her daughter Florida, she also started an important publication, *Woman's Era* magazine. She is credited with calling the first organizing convention of Black women, which resulted in the later calling of the first meeting of the National Association of Colored Women's Clubs.

Hallie Quinn Brown began her career as a teacher after having graduated from Wilberforce College in 1873. After a few years of teaching, she became very active in public speaking and traveled extensively as an elocutionist. After becoming well-known as an elocutionist, Brown returned to Wilberforce as a professor and again traveled extensively on behalf of the college. In addition to her many travels in America, she traveled to Europe (as did several other Black women at that time) where her ideas of universal suffrage and equal rights for African Americans were well-received. Strongly aligned with the Women's Christian Temperance Union and espousing their beliefs, Hallie Q. Brown played a prominent role in the push for national recognition by helping to set the national stage. Much later, she became the seventh president of the NACWC and served from 1920 to 1924.

Mary Church Terrell was one of the first women to be on a board of education in America and was the first African American woman to serve. She attended Oberlin College and in 1885 became a professor at Wilberforce College. Attending various suffrage group meetings, Terrell became very interested in women's clubs and would become a force well after the turn of the century. She served on a number of committees including the International Congress of Women, the International League of Peace, and the Women's International League of Peace and Freedom. She founded the College Alumnae Club and served as its first president. During World War I she served as the

National Supervisor of Work for the War Camp Community Service. She also served on the Republican National Committee. Unafraid to challenge other women's groups, Terrell led a fight against the American Association of University Women regarding its stance supporting school segregation. In part to indicate her defiance to some of the powerful male leaders of African Americans, she was a charter member of the National Association for the Advancement of Colored People. In 1896 she was elected first president of the National Association of Colored Women's Clubs. She was re-elected twice.

In 1892 Victoria Earle Mathews formed the Women's Loyal Union of New York and Brooklyn. Becoming its first president, Mathews worked tirelessly for morality, social justice, and education for African American women. She responded to the call made by Ruffin in 1895. As she did with her own club from 1892 to 1895, Mathews became an extremely active member of the NACWC, attending lectures, reading, and enjoining women to their causes. She served as chairperson of the executive board and as National Organizer for the NACWC. Some of her most enthusiastic work went into programs such as the Traveler's Aid Society, the White Rose Mission, kindergarten formation, community women's clubs, and the Home for Colored Working Girls. All of these initiatives focused on the moral and healthy care of young girls and women, especially those young girls and women alone in urban areas and subject to the prey of deceitful people.

Josephine Silone Yates was the only African American graduate of the Rhode Island State Normal School in 1879. She became an editorial writer for newspapers and wrote widely of numerous facets of life in America, including the lives of women. She established herself as a leader in the Kansas City Women's League in 1893. This involvement began her activity in local women's clubs. She used this local experience to become an avid supporter of the movement which led to the organization of the NACWC. Attending nearly every meeting and serving on

numerous committees, she played a large role in the national agenda and was elected as the organization's second president in 1900. At one point in her life she studied under Fannie Jackson Coppin.

Fannie Jackson Coppin graduated from Oberlin College in 1865. She began her teaching career at the Institute for Colored Youth in Philadelphia. Soon she became principal of the school and served in that capacity for 40 years. During that time of great educational/social change, she established the Women's Industrial Exchange, where the works of her students were displayed. She became involved in local women's clubs, spoke at NACWC national conventions, and took her place in history as a pioneer of the women's club movement.

Margaret Murray Washington attended Fisk University and began her teaching career in 1889 at Tuskegee Institute. Serving as both teacher and dean of women, Washington immersed herself in community work, home visitations, the comprehensive work of church and schools, and the ideas and philosophies of her future husband. After marrying Booker T. Washington, she established the Tuskegee Women's Club and served as its president for the rest of her life. As with many leading women of the club movement, her main focus was the perpetuation of high ideals for education and community life. Her endless work and popularity were pivotal in getting her elected as president of the Alabama State Federation of Colored Women. The goals of this organization were to support reform schools for Black boys, support schools for prisoners in jail, and support the establishment of schools for girls. Washington's work became well-known and supported across the South. She became president of the Federation of Southern Women's Clubs. She organized the International Council of Women of the Darker Races of the World. She became chairperson of the Interracial Commission of Alabama. Washington was also present at the organizational meeting of the NACWC and later served as its fifth president from 1912 to 1916.

Another early leader in the Black women's movement was Agnes Jones Adams. A member of the Women's Era Club, she also served in the organization of the meetings and proceedings that resulted in the formation of the NACWC. At the organizing meeting, Adams served as one of the presiding officers. In later meetings, she continued as a speaker for the national agenda for the Association of Colored Women's Clubs.

These early leaders in the nineteenth century and early twentieth century were the pioneers for the advancement of African American women's clubs. This advancement took place not only in the increasing of the numbers of local and state clubs, but in the forward movement toward national unity. These were the women who performed the most difficult groundwork of beginning the winds of change by going against the prevailing direction. They were students, teachers, abolitionists, writers, organizers, and leaders. They were fearless in a fearful endeavor. For women to be uniting in America to assert their rights and status was out of the mainstream. For African American women to be uniting in America to assert their rights and status was far, far out of the mainstream. The intelligence and perseverance these women incorporated in doing what they did led in the long run to the rise in personal/social status not only of themselves but for the masses.

History indicates the conditions that prevailed during the years after the Civil War. The dominant culture was not enthralled with emancipation and still considered African Americans an inferior race to the White population. Aside from the general daily discrimination by individuals, so-called Jim Crow laws were applied to keep the races separate not only on train cars and buses, but across the board in any public situation or accommodation. States passed laws against African Americans and laws that called for separation of the races. Indeed, a famous landmark federal court case was passed in 1895, *Plessy v. Ferguson,* which asserted that separate was equal. Oppression pervaded American society. The sum of the situation

in American society caused a trend for organization to develop among African Americans to deal with the racial pressures put upon them. In 1890, T. Thomas Fortune, editor of the *New York Age,* declared that African Americans must take hold of the problem themselves and address it so loudly that the world will realize the oppression and attempt to right the wrong (Wesely, 1984, pp. 24–25). Fortune set up a meeting which became known as the first organization for civic/political rights for African Americans. This organization, first named the Colored National League, became better known as the African American Council. Delegates from 23 states numbering over 120 individuals met in Chicago in 1890. A second meeting was held in 1891 in Nashville but by 1893 Fortune had to realize the organization was financially bankrupt and was without widespread support. In subsequent years, it was revived at times, but though it faded from the picture, it provided its purpose. Local organizations began to flourish to discuss, decide, and act on issues of civic/political importance to African Americans. T. Thomas Fortune had played his part and would continue to do so.

Other organizations of note were begun as well. In 1892, Booker T. Washington began the Tuskegee Conferences. The goals were to help Blacks attain success in their industrial, educational, moral, and religious lives. Washington would stay close to the development of Black women's clubs and attempted to deliver his ideas, especially on industrial education, as planks in the NACWC's platform. Also, in 1896 the National Association of Colored Men was formed in Detroit. The goal of this group was to oppose the Tuskegee Conferences as being too accommodating to the dominant culture. This was the main argument against Washington at the time. Some groups thought Washington was too accommodating to Whites. These groups wanted the immediate granting of full rights, including citizenship. They did not want to wait for rights while footholds in the economy were established. As with African American men, African American women took different sides of this issue.

As stated above, women had been organizing clubs on local levels and statewide in order to address local and state concerns. One of the earliest organizations was the Colored Women's League. This club was organized in the Washington, DC, area in 1892. The president was Helen Cook. In 1894 the Colored Women's League incorporated. Along with Cook, one of the members of the board to incorporate was Mary Church Terrell. The main stated goals of the club were to foster moral, intellectual, and social growth. The unstated goals were to drive for women's suffrage and equal rights. As always, the emphasis was on education to accomplish these goals. Night schools and kindergarten classes were established. An industrial committee was established to create programs in sewing, cooking, and gardening. All of these educational issues would become mainstays and more would be added. In addition, according to a Livingston County (Missouri) Library document entitled *Bicentennial Memories of Negroes*, it can be pointed out that as early as in 1893, Mary Church Terrell in an article in the *Afro-American Journal of Fashion* declared that the goal of the Colored Women's League was to bind together local clubs in a national organization (Williams, 1976).

A second key organization in the development of the birth of the NACWC was the Women's New Era Club of Boston. There were three leaders responsible for the establishment and leadership of this club. They were Josephine St. Pierre Ruffin, Florida Ruffin, and Maria Baldwin. The Women's New Era Club's purpose was to seek gifts of endowments with which kindergartens could be established. The group wanted to escalate the beginning of kindergarten so that it could encourage other groups to press the need for action in establishing the beginning of education along with education for mothers. Not only were those gifts obtained and kindergartens started in the Boston area, but gifts were attained in other areas that resulted in the establishment of kindergarten programs. One area of major success, for example, was Georgia. In addition, working from her position as president of the Women's New Era Club, Josephine St. Pierre Ruffin is credited with publishing and editing the first newspaper by an African American woman, *Woman's Era*. Actually an illustrated magazine, it was said to have accomplished more for the national club idea than any other source (Wesely, 1984, p. 26).

There were so many local clubs forming around the country that it was inevitable that locals began to think about and consider a national organization. They were already communicating with each other by word of mouth and letter. State organizations were forming and they themselves held conventions. It was nothing new to have people from several states at a state conference. These people would go back home to share ideas they had learned and to tell others what clubs were doing and what issues they were emphasizing. In addition, local and state organizations were putting out their own newsletters that were being shared as widely as possible. Furthermore, while all of this was going on, all African Americans, but in particular women, were aware that the Sorosis Club of New York had created a national organization of White women's clubs in 1892. African Americans took notice of this immediately and began to realize they would follow. It was now time for someone to take the lead and call for a national conference of African American women's clubs. This leadership came from Josephine St. Pierre Ruffin via the *Woman's Era* magazine of the Woman's New Era Club. Ruffin called the first national conference of colored women to Boston for July 29–31, 1895. The convention was originally named the First Congress of Colored Women, but when it actually took place it was re-named the National Federation of African American Women.

There were a couple of unique events in particular that spurred reasons for this first national meeting to be called. One came from what had to be one of the most action-inspiring editorials ever written. A man by the name of James W. Jacks, who was president of the Missouri Press Association, published an

article attacking colored women as "wholly devoid of morality and that they were prostitutes, thieves, and liars" (Wesely, 1982, p. 28). After decades of attempting to concentrate on educational, social, and especially moral uplifting, this was an attack that stung the women deeply and caused for action to be taken. Jacks had sent his article to the secretary of the Anti-Slave Society of New England, Florence Belgarnie. Belgarnie, indignant with Jacks's accusations, passed it on to the editors of the *Woman's Era* suggesting they publish the article in order to stir outrage at its accusations which would lead to action against Jacks and increased awareness of women's issues throughout the nation. Increased awareness, it was thought, would lead to increased public outcry for better conditions for women. When the editors received the article and letter Jacks had written, they deliberated before taking action. The two Ruffins and Maria Baldwin were unsure of the effects of re-publishing the article Jacks had written. They understood the reaction of outrage that would come from African Americans. They believed most but not all African Americans would rise up against Jacks's accusations. They also felt that some African Americans as well as the majority of Whites would accept the article as fact. What was decided in the end was that the article would not be re-published in fear of having people accept the content as true. Rather, in June of 1895, the editors chose in its magazine to describe carefully the article's contents in a review form. As expected, the description of Jacks's article riled people throughout the ranks who resented the accusations made by Jacks. The editors in response to the membership outcry sent copies of Jacks's letter to Belgarnie to clubs across the country. The copy of the letter from Jacks was accompanied by a letter from Josephine St. Pierre Ruffin. Not only did this accompanying letter respond to Jacks, it called for a historic event that would be pivotal in the formation of the National Association of Colored Women's Clubs. On June 1, 1895, Josephine St. Pierre Ruffin, President of the Women's New Era Club of Boston, issued a call for

convention to take place July 29–31, 1895.

In addition to the rousing incident of Jacks's letter, there was another more subtle but equally effective set of circumstances that gave escalated impetus to a national conference of African American women and the birth of the NACWC. As a traveling elocutionist, Hallie Quinn Brown had been journeying around the country (and in England) delivering speeches regarding equal rights, and especially citizenship and voting rights, for African American women. As she traveled about, she noticed that in nearly every place she went women were seeking her out to explain the need for more connections between and among African American women who were working for the rights of women. They saw Brown as an excellent example of coordinating people of similar thinking as she shared information from town to town. However, they expressed that she as one person was not enough and that she did not stay anywhere very long. The women did not feel that enough information was being shared in her visits. They also felt that there was not enough detail in what she was sharing and no plan for coordination of continued work with others. Enough women along her tour impressed upon her the need for closer relationships of women in order to be more productive in accomplishing the goals the women had for their local and state groups that she decided to think about it and do something about the concern. Brown decided to meet with the Washington, DC, based Colored Women's League to share what she had learned and to press for a national association. This meeting and Brown's influence with the members of the active and influential Colored Women's League fed into the stir of Jacks's letter and increased the motivation and desire to begin thinking about a national organization.

Thus, the call had gone out and clubs in various locations were ready to answer the call—and answer they did. A committee was formed, led by Josephine St. Pierre Ruffin, to plan the organizational meeting which assembled at Berkeley Hall, Boston, July 29,

30, 31, 1895. There were delegates from ten states in attendance and representatives from twenty clubs. There were also individual women from sixteen states and the District of Columbia who were there as independent, yet interested people. Indeed the call had gone out, and indeed it had been answered. The people in attendance understood the personal/social status of African American women in America and the oppression and discrimination that accompanied it. They had now joined together in a larger, more organized fashion than ever before to advance the causes of women's clubs. The program reflected the interest in the familiar issues of local and state clubs. In addition to the need for national organization, the following issues can be found in the original program:

- Industrial training for women
- Higher education enrollment and graduation for women
- Pleas for social/civic/moral justice
- Race literature
- Political equality
- Social purity
- Temperance
- Suffrage
- Citizenship

Both women and men addressed the convention on these and other issues. Some of the notable speakers included Josephine St. Pierre Ruffin (acting as president or presider at this organizational meeting), Helen Cook, Margaret Murray Washington, Victoria Earle Mathews, T. Thomas Fortune, Henry Blackwell, and William Lloyd Garrison. Ruffin gave the welcome and keynote speech of the conference. In it she celebrated the willingness and ability of African American women to do their part for the good of the people. On the second day of the meeting, Agnes Jones Adams gave an intriguing speech regarding social purity. This speech made a direct reference to the article Jacks had written and to the accusations he had made. On the third day of the meeting, the Committee on Resolutions, chaired by Ida Bell Wells

Barnett, advocated equality for all Black workers. High priority was also placed on home-making and home purchasing and the establishment of industrial schools. Mothers' meetings were proposed. An argument was presented against the withdrawal of federal troops in the South by President Hayes which had resulted in the increased mistreatment of African Americans. Heavy criticism of separate coach cars in Louisiana was addressed. The committee expressed a desire to have both parties condemn the practice of lynching (only the Republicans had done so).

Within the recommendations of the Committee on Resolutions, it is easy to see the influence of the prevailing social thought and philosophy within the Black community at the time. The recognized leader of African Americans at this point in time was Booker T. Washington. His emphasis on industrial training to join the workforce of the industrial revolution coincided with the women's clubs' quest for the higher education of women, though not exactly. It also coincided with the urge of education for children, though Washington's ideas were seen as limited. Washington also strongly believed in home-making and home-purchasing as a way to earn respect, be productive, and make a way into the economy. His main philosophy was to get African Americans working in the economy of the industrial revolution in order to lift themselves up financially. These were the first steps, he thought, to other rights and freedoms which would come later. As previously mentioned, there were two camps on this issue not only in African American culture in general, but also among African American women. Some wanted a push for immediacy of all rights. Some were willing to wait as Washington was. At a time during which women were attempting to gain power and influence, it is intriguing to observe how Booker T. Washington, the most powerful and influential African American of the time, monitors this group and influences its ideas and work. It is equally intriguing to observe how Washington's main adversary and future successor, W. E. B. Du Bois, manages his way

into the women's club groups and the NACWC in order to influence its ideas and work. It seems that the influence of both of these leaders, though necessary, did not bowl over the members of women's clubs to the extent that they lost their own identity and agenda. They were split on the men's two different philosophies but united, for the most part, on the main issues of the NACWC. This, it would seem, is a marvelous tribute to the dedication to cause and commitment to action that the women's groups possessed. Not being usurped by the tremendous power, especially of Washington, indicates the power that they themselves had earned through the hard work, organization, and righteousness of their cause. Booker T. Washington was at this first organizational meeting and would continue to attend biennial meetings. Though his speech at this organizational meeting in July of 1895 is not itemized, it is known that in September of 1895 he made his famous speech at the Atlanta Cotton States and International Exposition regarding accommodating the needed industrial workforce while waiting for personal/social freedoms (Johnson, 2002, p. 133). In addition, Washington arranged for a second conference to take place in December of 1895 in Atlanta. Called the Atlanta Conference of Colored Women, at this conference Washington reiterated his demands for African Americans that he had made in September stating that, "To earn a dollar in the factory just now is worth infinitely more than the opportunity to spend a dollar in the opera house" (Wesely, 1984, p. 35). Wesely reports that Washington's philosophy seemed to go unnoticed by this conference of women. It is relevant to note that at the 1895 organizational meeting Margaret Murray Washington, Booker's wife, gave a speech, entitled *Individual Work for Mental Elevation.*

This first national meeting of African American women, called the National Federation of African American Women (often referred to as the National Federation of Afro-American Women), elected Josephine St. Pierre Ruffin as its first president on the first day of the meeting. Also elected as officers were Helen Cook and Margaret Murray Washington as vice-presidents and Eliza Carter as secretary. It would seem that carrying her presidency from the Women's New Era Club and her work in making the call into her role as president at the National Federation of African American Women at this meeting would be logical for Ruffin and this group. She, after all, did the most to this point to get the momentum going. She is listed in the original program as president, and accounts of the meeting indicate she was directing the meeting. On its third day, however, Margaret Murray Washington was elected as president.

In 1896 the two best known established organizations for African American women met in Washington, DC, in back-to-back weeks. The Colored Women's League convention with Helen Cook as president met first. The many speakers at this convention included Fannie Jackson Coppin, Anna H. Jones, and Josephine Silone Yates. The speeches given were on the following topics:

- Establishment of kindergartens
- Industrial training for women
- Higher education for women
- Morality
- Careers for women
- Suffrage
- Citizenship

Several individual speeches were given on different careers such as nursing, teaching, writing, and business. These had become issues of prime importance and in fact addressed the issues that had been long at the forefront of the advancement of personal/social status for African American women. To get a foothold in the professions would establish a foothold in society.

During the week following the Colored Women's League convention, the Federation of African American Women met. President Margaret Murray Washington greeted the audience in attendance and gave the keynote speech. Among the other many

speakers at this conference were Helen Pitts Douglass (widow of Frederick Douglass) and Fannie Jackson Coppin. Main topics of discussion included prison reform, industrial training for women, and the elevation and improvement of domestic training, including motherhood and kindergarten. At this convention another historic event took place which would lead to the formation of the NACWC. A joint committee consisting of members of the Colored Women's League and the Federation of African American Women was created. This committee elected Mary Church Terrell as chair of the committee. It was this committee that made the resolution to join the two women's groups into one organization. The organization would be called the National Association of Colored Women. The resolution was put to the convention delegates for a vote. The resolution passed, the name was adopted, and after a full day of casting and re-casting ballots, Mary Church Terrell was elected president of the new national organization. To end this historic conference, a call went out for the first convention of the National Association of Colored Women for September 15–17, 1897. This organization is now known as the National Association of Colored Women's Clubs.

After the 1896 convention closed, means for broadening the awareness of the organization were sought. It was decided that the *Woman's Era* magazine would be the official mouthpiece of the NACWC (later to be replaced by *National Notes*). This was thought to be the logical way to spread the word of women's issues as well as to broaden the interest and involvement in order to establish a solid foothold in American society. In the August/September 1896 issue of *Woman's Era* an article appeared entitled, *First Statement as President of the National Association of Colored Women*. In this article Mary Church Terrell urged members, "to be forgetful of the past, hopeful of the future, and work in the present with undaunted courage and untiring zeal" (Wesely, 1984, p. 40). Other *Woman's Era* article topics in 1896 in preparation for the 1897 First Annual Convention included:

- Political and economic issues of the presidential election of 1896
- Education
- Women's issues, including suffrage and citizenship
- Paul Laurence Dunbar as a first-rate poet in the United States
- Legislation for colored people
- Appeals for the abolishment of discrimination
- Disapproval of *Plessy v. Ferguson* (This was compared to the Dred Scott Decision and antebellum days.)
- Announcement of a lecture to be given by Maria Baldwin to the Brooklyn Institute of Arts and Sciences. (This was the first time this institute had given an invitation to speak for the annual address.)

Other notable events of club women in 1896 included the establishment of an association to maintain the Frederick Douglass home. Douglass was high in stature to African American women because of his 1848 second to the motion to address women's right to vote and because of his lifelong work in the advancement of women's issues. History will show that the NACWC spent a tremendous amount of time, effort, and money in honoring Douglass throughout the years in appreciation for his role in uplifting the status of women. Another notable event was the establishment of a series of conferences under the leadership of W. E. B. Du Bois that resulted in the publication of the *Atlanta University Studies*. These publications were meant to espouse Du Bois's beliefs regarding his "talented tenth" and the betterment and uplifting of African Americans. Du Bois demanded immediacy of personal/social/civic rights for all Americans. This latter event, then, completes the inclusion of the two leading and competing African American males at this time and their differing, almost opposite, ideas into the women's movement. Both wanted to influence the NACWC to their way of thinking, and both spent considerable time attempting to win over the NACWC and its growing number of members.

The First Annual Convention of the NACWC was held in Nashville on September 15, 16, and 17, 1897. Sixty-three delegates from twenty-six clubs and many states attended. They were greeted by President Mary Church Terrell in her President's Speech, which concluded that the home is the main avenue for improvement and advancement of African Americans. The home meant family, relationships, child rearing, education, and jobs. Living morally was always defined in these ways as well as in affiliation with religion. The rest of the conference program featured discussion of the organization's constitution and goals and many speeches on popular topics. Some of the many speakers included Fannie J. Jackson, Lizzy Williams, and Susan Adams. The following were themes of the many speeches:

- The Frederick Douglass monument
- Convict release systems
- Separate car laws
- High moral standards
- Needs for mothers' meetings
- Education
- Kindergarten
- Temperance
- Suffrage
- Citizenship

Mary Church Terrell was re-elected as president. Francis Jackson Coppin, Josephine St. Pierre Ruffin, Francis Ellen Watkins Harper, Josephine Silone Yates, Sylvania Williams, Jennie Chase Williams, and Lucy Thurman were all elected as vice-presidents. Anna V. Thompkins and Alice Ruth Moore were elected secretaries. Mary Trisbee Handby was elected treasurer. Victoria Earle Mathews was elected as National Organizer. Margaret Murray Washington was elected as Chair of the Executive Board, and J. Napier Kemp was elected as chair of Ways and Means.

One important order of business was deciding on a constitution. In working through discussions for the NACWC constitution, many ideas were presented and, as would be expected, arguments over those ideas took place. Language was particularly con-

troversial. Discussion included the use of the phrase "by the help of God" as an important qualifier of guardianship. The motion to use this phrase was made by Lucy Thurman, and the motion was passed and adopted as part of the constitution. The usual membership requirements, program procedures, and voting procedures were included in addition to what The *African American Registry* reports would eventually become the long-lasting goals of the organization. Seven national goals adopted by the NACWC were the following:

1. To promote the education of women and children
2. To raise the standards of the home
3. To improve conditions for family living
4. To work for the moral, economic, social, and religious welfare of women and children
5. To protect the rights of women and children
6. To secure and enforce civil and political rights for the African American race
7. To promote interracial understanding so that justice may prevail among all people (*African American Registry*, 2005)

These goals essentially have survived the evolution of the organization and remain today, though stated in slightly altered verbiage and with some additions, as the objectives of the NACWC.

There was another order of business. The Resolutions Committee played an important and essential role at this first annual meeting. What resolutions would be passed would set the standards for future resolution committees and indeed the avenues of discussion important to delegates at future conferences. Five important resolutions adopted at the First Annual Convention of the NACWC were the following:

1. Clubs should petition state legislatures for the repeal of the separate car law
2. The Tennessee Industrial School was to be petitioned to give colored boys an equal chance to attend to learn trades

3. Endorsement of the establishment of the John Brown Industrial School, the Douglass Memorial Monument, and the establishment of homes for the aged and reformatories for delinquents should occur
4. Opposition to juvenile secret societies, crime, liquor trafficking, and lynching should be announced
5. Support and commendation for the Women's Christian Temperance Union should be made

The close of this historic First Annual Convention noted the location and date of the first biennial meeting to be Chicago in 1899. With the announcement of the first biennial meeting the NACWC was clearly showing its resiliency to the pitfalls of beginning a new organization. It had adopted a constitution, identified national goals, entertained affiliates from far and wide, elected officers, charted a future course, and set the location and date of its next meeting. All of this was accomplished in addition to the many speeches/presentations given that stimulated discussion of the very issues of most concern to club members. Indeed, it appeared that the National Association of Colored Women's Clubs was here to stay.

Having held the organizational meeting in 1896 and the First Annual Convention in 1897, the National Association of Colored Women's Clubs in 1899 held what was to become the First Biennial Meeting of the National Association of Colored Women's Clubs. Thus, a regular schedule (with limited alterations) of biennial meetings in different locations around the country has been in place since 1899 to the present. These meetings would continue the discussion of the national umbrella of issues related to local and state concern. In this way, the national association not only led the local and state club work via the national agenda, but listened to, took pride in, and supported the work of local and state clubs. A working relationship developed on all levels that led to a common philosophy and mission from which to gain personal, social, civil status,

rights, and privileges as well as first-class citizenship for all. The NACWC motto, *Lifting as We Climb*, stands as a symbol for as the club women gain, they lift the status of all people, in particular Black people, especially Black women. The motto was adopted with the intention of showing "an ignorant and suspicious world that our aims and interests are identical with those of all good, aspiring women" (*African American Registry*, 2005). In commenting on the motto, Mary Church Terrell wrote the club's members, "have determined to come in to the closest possible touch with the masses of our women, through whom the womanhood of our people is always judged" (Giddings, 1984, p. 98). Author Paula Giddings (1984) states in her writing of women's history that, "For these Black women, character was judged by where a woman wanted to go rather than where she was" (p. 98).

The 1899 Biennial Meeting of the National Association of Colored Women's Clubs convened in Chicago on August 14, 15, 16. President Mary Church Terrell opened the meeting with her welcome and review of the unfolding of the establishment of the NACWC. The gist of her comments was an enthusiastic expression that individual local and even state clubs could accomplish little alone, but they could accomplish much with the support and organization of a national association with a national agenda and a following of various parties of interest. Great accomplishments, she stated, would be achieved through the togetherness and connection and common goals of the national organization in conjunction with local and state branches. Terrell's remarks were well-received, and her enthusiasm was met with an equally enthusiastic response. Other opening remarks were made by several local business people who welcomed the delegates and representatives to Chicago. Booker T. Washington also addressed the opening of this conference. His welcome included, to be sure, his pitch for industrial education and the furthering of African American entry into the American industrial job market.

The formal program consisted of the presentation of papers by many notable women including Josephine Silone Yates, Carrie Fortune, Lucy Thurman, and Elizabeth Carter. Terrell, herself, delivered three speeches: *Convention Welcome, The Progress of Colored Women,* and *The Life of Harriet Beecher Stowe.* Josephine Silone Yates delivered a speech entitled, *Social Necessity of an Equal Moral Standard for Men and Women.* Other speeches provided more thoughts on the familiar topics of concern for NACWC: child rearing, convict release programs, labor questions, lynch laws, practical club work, kindergartens, equal moral standards for men and women, prison work, race literature, temperance reform, suffrage, and citizenship. One other presentation by Mary Church Terrell was printed and sold to delegates and representatives for ten cents each. This tactic was used so that people would not only have an interest in kindergarten, but they would have a plan from which to establish kindergarten. It also earned money for the club coffers. A speech by Josephine B. Bruce regarding the unequal treatment of Blacks and Whites by labor unions resulted in a resolution that demanded that labor unions stop their shortsighted and crude treatment of Blacks. A committee was formed to lobby union leaders for equal treatment. When it came time to elect a president for the next two years, several candidates vied for the position. Josephine B. Bruce, Margaret Murray Washington, Lucy Thurman, Josephine St. Pierre Ruffin, Mary Church Terrell, and Josephine Silone Yates all ran and received votes. The eagerness to serve was obvious. Mary Church Terrell was re-elected for the 1899–1901 biennial.

There were other events worth mentioning surrounding the First Biennial Meeting. W. E. B. Du Bois, in what seems to be more drama in the competition for influence with Booker T. Washington for a certain amount of ideological management of the NACWC, went out of his way during the meetings to publish overly flattering remarks. He was effusive in his praise for the intelligence, beauty, and culture of the women in attendance at the meeting. Jane

Addams of Hull House invited the delegates to a luncheon. The *Chicago Times Herald* reported that, "This was the first time that colored women have been given the decided recognition in a social way by a woman of lighter skin" (Wesely, 1982, p. 48). This event was seen as progress.

This 1899 Biennial Meeting rooted the NACWC as a national organization of prominence that was firmly established in American society and would remain so into the future. The election of officers from several different states enhanced the status of the organization and added to its recognition as permanent. The importance of this firm foundation is manifold. It gives impetus to universal recognition of crucial issues of African American women. It gives motivation, coordination, and direction to local and state clubs that follow the goals of the national organization. Clubs now were able to see a national vision that was much larger than local or state issues but still connected. Local and state groups felt good about being part of a bigger picture. In addition to all these benefits, a permanent, popular, influential, successful national organization also makes other national groups and individuals of influence pay attention to its ideas and goals and desires. To this end in this case, the leading national women's group until this point in time, the General Federation of Women's Clubs, was influenced by the success of the NACWC so that they recognized it as a viable organization and needed to consider its agenda. Realizing that these two organizations had some common interests, the president of the state delegation of Georgia to the Fifth Biennial Convention of the General Federation of Women to be held in Milwaukee asked Josephine St. Pierre Ruffin to attend. However, when Ruffin agreed and registered, a problem developed. It was suggested that she register only as a member from White clubs and not as a member of the Black Women's New Era Club. When Ruffin insisted upon being registered as a member of the Women's New Era Club, an argument ensued. Refusing to back down, Ruffin escalated her demands that not only she be accepted on the basis of her gen-

der (not race), but that the Women's New Era Club be accepted on the basis of its business, not because of the race of its members. This insistence triggered a heated debate with resolutions in favor of and against Ruffin's demands. Northern delegates urgently requested that the federation drop race issues and allow the two demands. Southern delegates insisted on White-only language to be made even more clearly written into the constitution. Ballots went back and forth. In the end, Ruffin was not recognized as a delegate nor was the New Era Club recognized.

Reaction to the exclusion of Ruffin and the Women's New Era Club presented some interesting ideas. First, the exclusion of African Americans from the General Federation of Women inspired, renewed, and re-invigorated the efforts of the NACWC. This, by extension, re-doubled the efforts of local and state clubs to work toward their goals. Second, this circumstance helped to diffuse the idea put forth by White people and resented by the African Americans that they wanted to keep separate from White people, to keep to their own. Clearly, Blacks wanted to join Whites in mutual work and progress, but Whites refused to cooperate. Finally, a related incident summarized the thoughts and feelings of African Americans regarding the refusal of their acceptance into the General Federation of Women. Before the convention, a Black women's club from Racine, Wisconsin, made application to attend the Fifth Biennial Convention of the General Federation of Women. The club was told that the application had been received too late. In response, R. H. Anderson, President of the Racine Phyllis Wheatley Club stated, "This is an old fight all over again. Years ago the men in the South fought our men. Now the women are fighting us" (Wesely, 1982, p. 50). A year later in 1900 the General Federation of Women changed its constitution to allow African American women full rights as delegates. Ruffin had taken a stand that caused change and made a difference in the progress of African American women, all women, all people.

Progress then. Progress now. The National Association of Colored Women's Clubs began in

1896 as a method to make a difference. By 1900, that difference was being seen. For the next 105 years more barriers would fall, more opportunities would be developed, and more people of all colors would benefit. Enough? No. However, without the National Association of Colored Women's Clubs where would we be now?

Glossary

Assimilation—A term used to describe dominated or minority cultures taking on the values and lifestyles of the dominant culture.

Atlanta (Southern) Compromise—Said to be the result of a speech given by Booker T. Washington that promoted industrial education for African Americans.

Censorship—The debate over whether the movie industry or the federal government should censor television and movies to ensure the proper development of children.

Efficiency Movement—The successor of the Progressive Movement, this movement used scientific methods to make schools more operationally and instructionally efficient.

Industrialization—As factories and manufacturing developed, this term was used to describe the transition from an agrarian society into an industrial society.

League of United Latin American Citizens—This organization was established in the twentieth century to identify and promote issues of Latin Americans living in the United States.

National Association for the Advancement of Colored People—The association was established in the early twentieth century to identify and promote issues of African Americans.

Progressive Reform Movement—A movement of prominence in the early twentieth century that addressed issues such as labor regulations, corruption in politics, democratic government, urban living conditions, and education.

Schools as Social Centers—An idea by John Dewey in the early twentieth century that suggested to connect school and work with school being the hub of the community.

Scientific Method—This phrase is broadly defined as a system of measuring time management and cost effectiveness to arrive at standard operations for efficiency.

Social Efficiency Doctrine—This doctrine suggests to promote the teaching of cooperation within the differentiated curriculum to accommodate the social needs of students.

Social Reconstruction—Born out of a speech by progressive George Counts in 1932, this concept promoted schools as the institution for reconstructing a healthy economic society.

Taylorism—Scientific methods applied to factories and schools.

Urbanization—The growth of cities in the nineteenth century as a result of industrialization and immigration.

Review

1. Describe the social, economic, and political factors that dominated this era.
2. To what does the Southern Compromise refer?
3. Explain Taylorism.
4. Explain the progressive point of view.
5. Describe the emphasis on industrial education in this era.
6. Describe the comprehensive school movement.
7. Explain *Plessy v. Ferguson*.
8. Explain the evolving concepts of republicanism, nationalism, patriotism, and Americanism.
9. You are a southern industrialist wanting to build a factory. What will you do?
10. Which two factors stand out in this era, and why?
11. Explain social efficiency and the concept of school as a social center.
12. Describe the Jazz Age, women's liberation attempts, and Prohibition.
13. Explain the ideas of John Dewey.
14. What school decisions were made to develop nationalism and Americanism during this era?
15. Describe programs developed to help get America out of the Depression.
16. It is 1925 and you are a parent of two teenagers: one girl and one boy. What discussions will you have with your children?
17. What do you think are the main changes that occur when a society goes from agricultural to industrial?
18. Compare and contrast women's liberation of the 1920s with that of today.
19. Compare and contrast patriotism of the early 1900s with that of today.
20. Are children better off in in the early twenty-first century than they were in the 1920s?

Selected Topics for Further Study

1. African American education to 1920
2. Mexican American education to 1920
3. Asian American education to 1920
4. Native American education to 1920
5. The purposes of public schools to 1920
6. Censorship of movies, radios, and television programming
7. Prohibition
8. Women's rights
9. The Jazz Age
10. Flappers
11. The Depression
12. The New Deal
13. President Hoover
14. President Roosevelt
15. The Bonus Army
16. Social Security
17. Federal Deposit Insurance Corporation
18. The automobile history of the 1920s, 1930s, 1940s
19. The stock market
20. Auguste Rodin

CHAPTER FOUR

Education and World Power

Patriotism, Civil Unrest, Renewed Patriotism

Post-war America saw a booming economy. "Good times are here again!" seemed to be the mantra of this era in its beginning stages. Industry was again producing domestic products which were rapidly sought after by confident consumers. Employment and the economy were major boom areas, especially in industries such as auto manufacturing, related auto industries, freeway construction, fashion, food, hygiene, home building, and entertainment. By 1944 school enrollment was at 5.5 million children, and the **baby boom** continued to increase attendance for the next three decades. From 1946 to 1956 alone, school enrollments increased 37% as a result of the baby boom (Webb, 2006, p. 262). One area of concern was that of how to provide employment for returning military veterans while maintaining the steady youth employment that had been increased during the war. Two major ways of dealing with this concern were the G. I. Bill of Rights of 1944 and the Universal Military Training and Service Act of 1951. The G. I.

Baby boom
The increased number of human births between 1944 and 1964

Bill of Rights (also known as the Serviceman's Readjustment Act) was designed to lessen the impact on a flooding labor market by encouraging returning veterans to attend school rather than go right into the workforce. It provided monetary motivation for returning veterans to go to college, thus lightening the job market crunch. Thousands of military veterans took advantage of this legislation by going to universities, colleges, and technical or vocational schools. Tuition, books, and other expenses were paid for by the federal government. Many educators later concluded that this bill, though extremely popular, swelled the ranks of colleges and reduced the value of a college degree. It did, however, serve its purpose to reduce the crunch in the labor market.

The Red Scare

The Universal Military Training and Service Act of 1951 was not as much involved with the labor market as it was about increasing the numbers of engineers and scientists needed to combat Communism and providing a strong military to help America remain a world power. The debate regarding universal military training was, in fact, not about whether or not there should be military training but, rather, about who should be exempt from it. Leading American scientists such as Vannevar Bush and James B. Conant supported plans for scientists and engineers to be exempt from military training. They called for 75,000 deferments per year for people to study science in order to end poverty, save the environment, improve national health, and develop national security (Spring, 2001a, p. 362). One result of these scientists' efforts was the creation of the National Science Foundation in 1950. Colleges and universities feared reduced enrollment, leading to budget problems, if everyone had to serve. The military itself did not want to take men they did not think were qualified. After vigorous debate and evidence submitted by a number of leading scientists, military men, and various academicians, as well as groups such as the Committee on the Present Danger,

the Universal Military Training and Service Act of 1951 was passed. The primary content of the bill called for the president to authorize deferments for those whose academic study was necessary to national health, safety, or security. Local draft boards were given the power to grant deferments based on the federal legislation or their own guidelines. At the time, scientists, universities, and the military were all satisfied with the aims of the bill. Clearly, all three entities were accommodated in their quest for the populations they desired. The numbers of scientists and engineers increased, the military remained strong, and the college enrollments rose. Unfortunately, in the long run this legislation also caused a flood in college enrollment, which resulted in a decline in the value of a college degree on the job market.

Furthermore, the split between professional educators and business that occurred during the Depression widened. Business and military people keenly observed the Russians developing an aerospace industry and, in 1949, testing the A-bomb. They linked these events to the establishment of Russian military power. This development began to threaten the American notion of the United States as a world power. As an alert went up from this and other escalating fears, the **Cold War** began, and the United States and Russia began monitoring each other's weapons and forms of government.

Cold War

The period after World War II during which Russia and the United States monitored each other

By the early 1950s, fear of Russian Communism was again identified as the (second) Red Scare, both in society and in schools. The conservatives announced that schools were being run by Communists. They wanted to remove all anti-American literature from school curricula and libraries as well as fire all "left-leaning" teachers. The fear of Communism caused schools and society to mistrust one another, and leaders in the business sector, who demanded that schools and administrators be reviewed, blamed the threat of Communism on ineffective schools led by ineffective administrators. As if a symbol of the Red Scare, the Korean War was

fought from 1950 to 1953. This reality added fuel to the fear and resulted in conservative accusations from such people as Allen Zoll of the National Council for American Education, historian Arthur Bestor, and Navy Admiral Hyman Rickover that the educational system and schools specifically were anti-intellectual. They claimed that schools were the weakest link in the fight against Communism, blamed liberals, and called for loyalty oaths from text-book writers, a national curriculum devoted to math, science, history, English, and foreign language, and the removal of un-American textbooks (Webb, 2006, p. 263). Senator Joe McCarthy added his indictment of schools as soft on Communism and broadened his attack to include notable social celebrities, politicians, and military people as Communists working to undermine the American democracy. Liberal educators bore the brunt of the Red Scare and remained the targets of right-wing conservative ideologues to the present (Webb, 2006, p. 270).

Other factors in addition to the Red Scare impacted schools at this time. The post-war baby boom led to an increased population which in turn caused a rise in school attendance and a shortage of facilities, teachers, curriculum, and methodological innovations. While struggling with these problems, schools were suddenly confronted with the culmination of Communist fear when on October 4, 1957, Russia sent *Sputnik* up into space and Americans united in a collective gasp in fear of a Communist takeover. President Eisenhower immediately proposed legislation to upgrade the math, science, and foreign language curricula in U.S. public schools for the purposes of catching up with and surpassing Russia in the **space race.** The National Defense Education Act was quickly passed in 1958, delivering millions of dollars to public schools for the expressed categorical areas of math, science, and foreign language in order to help the United States catch up with Russian technology, beat off any Communist infiltration, and remain a world power. Combined with the passage of the National Science

Space race

The competition between the Soviet Union and the United States to lead the world in technology by developing space programs

Foundation created in 1950, this act added tremendous momentum to the teaching of math, science, and foreign language. The differentiated curriculum of the comprehensive school movement gained momentum as increased sorting and training of students for human capital was heightened in the fight against Communism. The National Defense Education Act became a means by which the federal government could control local educational policy by controlling funding. In this regard, the federal government solidified its role as a national curriculum developer.

Dominated Cultures and the Continued Quest for Civil Rights

While these efforts to fight Communism were continuing, other social and political factors were also influencing schooling and society. Minority populations continued their fight against segregation and oppression both in schools and in society. In a 1948 case, *Delgado v. Bastrop Independent School District,* segregated Mexican education was judged illegal. In the 1954 case, *Brown v. Board of Education of Topeka,* segregation was found to be inherently unequal. These cases, especially *Brown,* escalated the quest for civil rights in America. However, by 1955 these laws were still not being enforced. Politicians and lawmakers were ignoring equalization laws in fear of not being re-elected by a still racist society. For these reasons, *Brown II,* sometimes called the "Enforcement Decree," was passed to end segregation "with all deliberate speed," as *Brown* had originally intended. By the end of 1955, with White people still rejecting the enforcement decree, Rosa Parks sat in the front of a Montgomery bus, thus initiating what became a year-long bus strike in Montgomery, Alabama. African Americans were asserting their quest for social justice.

Before *Sputnik* went up in 1957, there was social upheaval in Little Rock, Arkansas, as Governor Orval E. Faubus refused to allow African American students to attend Central High School. In an unparalleled occurrence, President Eisenhower found it

necessary to send the National Guard to Little Rock to counter the Arkansas State Guard and enforce the federal law to integrate the school. After days and weeks of ugly confrontation, the school was integrated by November. In 1958 Governor Faubus closed the school in retaliation (Schuman, 2004, p. 82).

From 1958 to 1963 the nation saw marches, sit-ins, protests, demonstrations, freedom rides, and a plethora of other events all meant to establish the social justice of equal rights, and all met with fierce resistance from the dominant culture. The nation, especially in the South, was in a state of social change. In 1963, Martin Luther King marched on Washington to deliver his best remembered "I Have a Dream" speech. He affected not just African Americans and their quest for social justice but other oppressed populations who were inspired by King and his cause to escalate their own battles. Indeed, White Americans began joining the cause for equal rights for all Americans in larger numbers.

However, a leader in the equal rights campaign, President John F. Kennedy, was assassinated in 1963. Interpretation of evidence surrounding the assassination remains controversial, and one result was a renewed visit to the Communist scare as the apparent assassin, Lee Harvey Oswald, was linked to the Russian government. Among other results, the space race escalated. In an effort to bolster the country's confidence in overcoming Communism, President Kennedy boldly announced in 1960 that America would land a man on the moon by the end of the decade. While casualties occurred in this race, it culminated in Americans landing on the moon in July of 1969. In effect, this event determined America as the technological leader of the world. It should also be noted that two landmark court cases were passed in 1962 (*Engel v. Vitale*) and in 1963 (*Abington School District v. Schempp*) that rebuffed attempts by conservatives to allow prayer and Bible study in public schools. These cases became the cornerstones of debate regarding religion in public schools for decades and led to many more court cases.

Civil Rights, Two Wars, and Progress
for Dominated Cultures

Huge social and political events begin merging by 1964. The passage of the colossal Civil Rights Act of 1964 was a major step in the progress toward civil rights for all Americans in the areas of employment, voting rights, public accommodations, and education. This act extended the powers of federal legislation to impact civil rights and education by using money to control educational policy. At the same time the first protests against the war in Vietnam began at the University of California—Berkeley. And continuing the work of John F. Kennedy as described in the *Heller Report,* President Lyndon Johnson began to wage another important war that attracted increasing attention and called for schools as the major influence in overcoming a societal problem. President Johnson announced his "War on Poverty" leading to the passing, in 1965, of the Elementary and Secondary Education Act, which provided millions of dollars for educationally deprived children in poverty. President Johnson was dubbed the modern Horace Mann. By this time, poverty and discrimination were both seen as interfering with the sorting and training for human capital within the comprehensive school's differentiated curriculum. The concern was that poverty and discrimination would prevent the discovery of talent for use in the national economy and for defense purposes. The War on Poverty was meant to remedy that influence.

From 1965 to 1975 social upheaval continued to escalate on all three levels. War protestors continued their demonstrations. California, Michigan, Wisconsin, and Ohio campuses became symbols of anti-war sentiments as demonstrations became violent. On May 4, 1970, four students died at Kent State University and, although people against the war remained active, violent demonstrations ceased, and Kent State was recognized as the end of violent protests. The War on Poverty became more difficult as President Richard Nixon took office in 1968 and reduced funding for the poor. President Nixon

encouraged the idea that the federal government should not be involved with funding programs for the disadvantaged. In 1965 a new immigration act passed, replacing the 1924 Immigration Act, and spurring on the continuing quest for civil rights as new populations came to the United States. Throughout the 1960s and well into the late 1980s, multicultural education was recognized as a significant educational concept. In the struggle for civil rights, two more important leaders were lost in 1968. Martin Luther King was gunned down in April, and in June Robert Kennedy was slain.

Dominated cultures made some gains in this era. Throughout the 1960s and 1970s the federal government gave support to Native Americans for self-determination. In 1966 Navajo parents participated in establishing the Rough Rock Demonstration School to preserve Native American languages and cultures. Throughout the 1960s groups such as the **Pan Indian Movement and American Indian Movement** formed to preserve Indian rights. There were demonstrations as well. In 1968 President Nixon supported the right of self-determination for Native Americans. In 1969 the United States Senate report *Indian Education: A National Tragedy* called for an end to the forced assimilation and cited sixty specific recommendations for doing so. In 1969 Indians took over Alcatraz, demanding recognition of Indians who had been cheated out of their land, and in 1972 the March of the Trail of Broken Treaties converged on Washington. The Bilingual Education Act passed in 1968, creating federal funds for the development of programs that teach both Native languages and English, and in 1972 the Indian Education Act passed, funding school programs for Native American culture and also establishing the Office of Indian Education. The **Chicano Movement** from 1965 to 1975 pressed for Chicano studies in colleges and resulted in lower dropout rates and increased educational attainment. In 1967 the **Mexican American Legal Defense Education Fund** (MALDEF) was established to protect students who

---

Pan Indian Movement and American Indian Movement

Organizations formed in the 1960s to preserve the rights of Indians

---

Chicano Movement

A movement prominent from 1965 to 1975 to press for Chicano studies in colleges and universities

---

Mexican American Legal Defense Education Fund

An organization established in 1967 to protect the rights of students punished for their involvement in civil rights issues

La Raza Unida

An organization established in 1967 to protect the rights of Mexican Americans and to preserve their language and culture

Magnet schools

Specialty schools within a district to offer alternative school programs to encourage voluntary integration

Alternative, charter, and choice schools

Contemporary offshoots of magnet schools, they offer specialized education as an alternative to public schools

were punished for being involved with civil rights issues. MALDEF broadened its scope to take on other issues such as funding. Another group, **La Raza Unida**, was also established in 1967 to protect the rights of Mexican Americans and preserve their language and culture. In a 1971 court case brought about by MALDEF, *Rodriguez v. San Antonio Independent School District,* funding for Mexican American education was granted, only to be taken away in the overturning of this case in 1973. In 1970, another MALDEF case, *Cisneros v. Corpus Christi Independent School District,* concluded that Mexican Americans were a federally identified dominated culture. The impact of this case was to recognize Mexican Americans as being included in the *Brown* decision. In 1974 *Lau v. Nichols,* based on rights for Asian Americans, was passed, guaranteeing equal education to non-English speaking students. In 1975 the Indian Self-Determination and Educational Assistance Act, which gave tribes the power to contract with the federal government for Native American education and health programs, was passed. These all serve as examples of continued advances in the causes of oppressed populations and attempts to achieve equal rights.

As 1975 drew to a close, however, the emphasis on equal rights seemed to be diminishing as other court cases came to the fore. Researcher James Coleman concluded a study which claimed that involuntary school segregation was causing White flight and thus increasing segregation. Busing laws for integration such as *Swann v. Mecklenburg* (1971) and *Milliken v. Bradley* (1974) created violent protests as Whites still rejected minority populations and the idea of school integration. **Magnet schools** were created to offer attractive school programs to encourage voluntary integration. Begun in the early 1970s, by the 1980s and 1990s, these magnet schools transitioned into **alternative, charter, and choice schools**. In addition, a new and growing set of issues revolved around gender equity and educational rights for the handicapped. Indeed, in this period two

lasting controversial laws (among others) were passed, one regarding gender equity (Title IX of the Higher Education Act of 1972) and one regarding rights for the handicapped (PL 94–142, 1975). The National Organization for Women and the Pennsylvania Association for Retarded Children were beginning to make their marks.

In 1968 Richard Nixon was elected president primarily on the promise to end the Vietnam War and to restore law and order in America. Americans wanted an end to the liberal government and society of the 1960s. The civil rights movement that had worked for individual rights and freedoms resulted in a dominant culture backlash. President Nixon opposed the War on Poverty, legislation for the poor, and busing for integration. He promoted career education, a back-to-basics curriculum, accountability, and the expansion of vocational education. Sidney Marland, Nixon's commissioner of education, called for career education as a reform movement which would restore order by ending rebellion, delinquency, and unemployment. Thus, from 1970 to 1973 career education was a focal point in education. The accompanying accountability movement was meant to restore power to the experts and take it away from local administrators. The heart of the accountability movement included standardized achievement tests with scores being reported to the public in order to identify school performance on tests and then to criticize or praise schools based on these results. Taking the opportunity to appoint four conservative members of the Unites States Supreme Court, Nixon was better able to accomplish his educational and other goals for America. By the end of the 1970s, attempts to integrate began to decrease (Webb, 2006, p. 286).

The war in Vietnam came to an end with the fall of Saigon in 1975. Americans tried to recover before new wars for America broke out around the world, especially after 1980. These wars continued to influence school curricula as Americans decided whether to support them. Meanwhile, the federal govern-

ment influenced school policy by passing laws that sought to establish national unity within the realm of the dominant culture.

President Carter: 1977–1981

In the evolution of education, this brief Carter era brings two clear issues into play regarding political and religious factors. These will be discussed below. During his time in office, President Jimmy Carter added eight million jobs to the economy, decreased the national deficit, and appointed record numbers of women, African Americans, and Hispanics to government jobs (Bourne, 1997). Thus, economic, philosophical, and social factors came under consideration as well.

Carter and Teachers Unions: The Deal

Teacher unions, first formed in 1857, had been gaining momentum since the 1950s in their influence on working conditions, teachers' rights, and teacher contracts. By the 1960s and into the 1970s teacher unions were called militant after a number of testy and sometimes violent strikes had occurred across the country, most notably in New York and Wisconsin. With its growing ranks and improved organization, the National Education Association (NEA) sought more ways to establish its power base to obtain the gains it hoped for in education. It found an answer in presidential politics. The NEA struck a deal with candidate Carter: in return for NEA endorsement, Carter, if elected, would create the U.S. Department of Education. When Carter was elected, he fulfilled that promise and created the Department of Education, appointing a woman, Shirley Hufstedler, to run it. This deal led to recognition of the NEA's power in influencing political elections. From this time forward political figures sought to claim themselves as the educational candidate in order to gain the support of the now powerful NEA. This logically resulted in the NEA's attempt to ideologically manage candidates on educational issues, as they have

done ever since. In addition, with its own cabinet-level department, education received official recognition as a central concern in America. Access to more resources, including a federal budget line, also gave educators increased power and prestige. Perhaps most importantly, the United States Secretary of Education would now manage the administration's educational agenda from the bully pulpit of the United States Department of Education. From an educational point of view, this makes the Carter administration a milestone in the evolution of American education. An increased national awareness of educational issues and candidates seeking NEA support gave rise to the interest in American education.

President Carter favored bilingual education in particular and other measures for the re-introduction of the federal government into educational programs. Carter increased the federal role in education mainly through increased federal funding for schools, especially in the areas of programs for minorities and the handicapped. Both the NEA and the other national teachers union, the American Federation of Teachers, supported President Carter and the Democratic Party. This support forced Carter's Republican opponent in the 1980 election to look elsewhere for support. As education was a strong issue in the 1976 campaign, especially public education and teachers' unions, and led to the election of President Carter, the next presidential candidate wanted to take advantage of the national interest in education while at the same time separating himself from the sitting president.

Republican Opposition to Carter and the Unions

Candidate Ronald Reagan and the Republican Party understood that there had to be an educational platform of some kind in order to be the education candidate. With education established as a vote-getting important issue, and with the knowledge that Republicans would not get the union vote, they decided to appeal to groups that opposed teachers' unions and were critical of public schools. These

groups included private and parochial schools looking for federal money via vouchers and tax credits. These groups also included Christian values groups such as the Moral Majority, who were most interested in support for school prayer and Bible study in public schools. Candidate Reagan promised all of the above and more and won the election in 1980.

The Reagan Years: 1981–1993

The choice school movement, which first began appearing in the 1970s as a conservative reaction to the liberal 1960s and early 1970s, found a great friend in President Ronald Reagan. Elected in both 1980 and 1984, President Reagan wooed the religious right and other conservatives, sometimes called the Christian Coalition, in his support for school prayer, school choice, and moral values for public schools. He also vowed to decrease and limit federal involvement in education. In particular, his goals, sometimes called the New Federalism, were to eliminate support for bilingual education, abolish the Department of Education, pass laws to allow prayer and Bible study in public schools, reduce funding for the handicapped, the impoverished, and minorities, and promote both public and private school choice programs by providing increased funding, vouchers, and tuition tax credits. President Reagan also wanted to establish the control of education at the state and local levels. He agreed with President Nixon that more business involvement with schools should occur (Schuman, 2004, p. 241).

Though President Reagan was unsuccessful in his attempts to dismantle the Office of Education, he drastically reduced its funding in order to reduce its power and prestige. This double reduction helped create his goal of decreasing the prestige of public education. The bully pulpit for public education was thus eliminated. His efforts in these areas solidified major differences between the Republican and Democratic parties. Republicans became the party of pro-private school measures, increased religion in public schools, and anti-union stances, while the Democrats

continued to support public schools, separation of church and state, and pro-union stances.

The Attack on Public Education

To bolster the attack on public education, the Reagan administration published *A Nation at Risk* in 1983. This publication blamed schools for the economic difficulties the United States was having in world markets. The report was particularly critical of the blandness of school curricula, of low expectations for grades, of too little time spent on academic subjects, and of the quality of teachers and teacher training. Because of his promise of reduced federal involvement in education, Reagan expected state and local agencies to correct the problems cited in *A Nation at Risk*. Foreseeing funding requests in the solution to this problem, the Republicans wanted to increase the state's role so that their promise of reduced federal control could be kept. With this shift to increased state control came a decline in local control, a pattern which continued for the next 30 years as states mandated educational rules to abide by federal mandates and locals took on the task of meeting state standards (Webb, 2006, pp. 323–325).

Another 1983 government report, *Action for Excellence*, called for a deeper alliance between schools and business. This push resulted in such programs as Adopt-a-School, Education for Employment, and School-to-Work Initiative. The idea was to draw business and schools closer to narrow the widening gap of U.S. economics in the world markets. The philosophical belief underlying this report was that schools should conform to business interests and seek business alliances.

The school reform issues that began shortly after President Reagan was elected focused on a top-down corporate formula for success: clear goals and high standards to produce a quality product (students). This **business model** consisted of a state level focus on school mandates and was popular through late 1985 and early 1986. By 1986 the Reagan administration had determined that schools were most ineffective

Business model
School reform established in the 1980s that focused on a top-down corporate formula for success

at the local level, and, thus, a state-level approach did not work. The new plan was to fix schools at the local level. The business model stayed in place; however, now it used a bottom-up rather than a top-down managerial style. By 1988 the additional problem of a national teacher shortage resulted in more controversy over alternative routes to certification (Webb, 2006, p. 322).

In the end, President Reagan successfully consolidated federal grants for education and proposed reduced spending for education in every budget request he made. From 1980 to 1989, federal funding for elementary and secondary education was reduced by 17%. Federal funding for higher education was reduced by 27% (Webb, 2006, pp. 322–323).

President George H. W. Bush, elected in 1988, carried on all aspects of the Reagan administration adding federal persuasion and funding to support additional concepts such as model schools, national standards, voluntary national achievement testing, and incentives for parental choice. These concepts became national goals out of the 1989 Governor's Conference. They set the stage for increased business partnerships, establishment of national and then state educational standards, mandatory achievement testing, and private choice programs. These changes resulted in increased federal mandates at state cost and reduced local control at a time when Republicans, led by Reagan and Bush, were calling for reduced federal involvement in education and increased local control. This decrease in federal funding left local municipalities and districts unable to support public education and supported the Republican agenda of promoting private and parochial education. In other words, when public education was unable to support itself because federal funds were taken away, private and parochial education would flourish by drawing in the former public school students. In the short run, President Bush could not get these national standards passed. In the long run, however, the effects of this plan would lead to the passing of a 2001 federal law calling for clos-

ing of public schools that fail to accomplish annual yearly progress toward standardized test scores. President Bush also created the National Council on Educational Standards and Tests, and he proposed voluntary achievement tests for grades 4, 8, and 12 (Schuman, 2004, pp. 241–242).

In the face of Republican efforts to do away with bilingual education, in 1983 a group calling itself **U.S. English** was established. The purpose of this group was to establish English as the national language. Between 1983 and 1988, this group encouraged fourteen states to declare English as their official language and inspired the conservative right to press for English-only school curricula and support services. This goal reflected the 100% Americanization programs in the history of education. Bilingual and multicultural education were attacked as unnecessary and irrelevant. Assimilation into the dominant culture was the theme for dominated cultures. In spite of these efforts, multicultural education leaders such as James Banks (Banks & Banks, 1989), Carl Grant and Christine Sleeter (Grant & Sleeter, 1986) continued to empower oppressed populations by integrating the history and culture of dominated groups into school curricula and textbooks. Two important pieces of legislation passed which assisted Native Americans—the Tribally Controlled Schools Act of 1988, which provided federal grants to fund tribal schools, and the Native American Language Act of 1990, which sought to preserve, protect, promote, practice, and develop Native American languages.

The relationship between business and schools continued to be strained. While workers wanted increased wages, business wanted lower wages. This issue especially concerned the lower and middle classes because the increasing inequality in the distribution of income paralleled the increasing inequality of educational opportunity. Poverty continued to escalate while federal programs and funding for impoverished populations decreased. By 1990, the wealthiest 20% of Americans had increased their income by 9% since 1977 while the poorest 20% had

U.S. English

Established in 1983, this group had as its goals the ending of bilingual education and English as the national language

experienced a 5% reduction in income (Spring, 2001a, p. 433).

The Last Democrat: 1993–2001

The conservative Republican rule was temporarily halted in 1992 when then moderate Democrat William Jefferson Clinton was elected to the presidency. President Clinton is said to have been elected to quell the rise in conservative politics and was looked upon as a liberal by conservative groups, such as the so-called Christian Coalition. These groups accused President Clinton of favoring too many federal programs for individual groups such as people in poverty. He also did not appear to do enough for non-public education agendas such as federal funding for private schools. In the end, liberals would look upon Clinton as a conservative whose federal programs for disadvantaged populations were neither substantial enough nor strong enough. They also felt he failed to fight the conservative agenda and adopted too many conservative ideas, such as educational standards and increased testing. President Clinton, who was in favor of increased federal involvement in education, promoted an agenda advocating more programs, more federal funding, and more enthusiasm for public education.

National Standards, the Secretary of Education, and School Choice

Having worked on national standards as a governor while chairing the 1989 Governors' Committee on Education, President Clinton supported national standards for education and went so far as to establish the National Board of Professional Teaching Standards. Possibly linked to these standards was his support for increased testing to hold students and teachers accountable for learning. President Clinton did not substantially change the direction of educational policies, but his administration was the most productive in terms of attention to education since the President Lyndon Johnson years (Webb, 2006, pp.

334–345). In his agenda for education he:

- Did not support religious rights in public schools
- Did not support public school prayer
- Did not support private school choice
- Supported school/business partnerships
- Supported funding for violence protection programs
- Supported increased funding for Head Start
- Supported career training
- Supported programs for increased equality of education
- Supported public school choice
- Supported the concept of national standards
- Supported increased spending on public education

President Clinton supported President Bush's Goals 2000 program and eventually signed into law the Goals 2000 Educate America Act in 1994. This act was yet another extension of the comprehensive school movement notion of sorting and training for human capital to catapult the United States to economic world power. It linked businesses with schools in an attempt to directly link school curricula to jobs. It increased federal funding for Head Start as well as pre-school and adult learning. The act was premised on the idea of education for lifelong learning. This further linking of schools to business resulted in several pieces of legislation being passed such as the 1994 School-to-Work Opportunities Act, which granted federal funds for schools with both school-based and work-based programs for education for employment. Career exploration and guidance, co-operative and on-the-job training programs, and connecting academic work to employment skills were major aspects of the act. These two major pieces of legislation became the main focal points of the Clinton administration. They represent a turning point in federal and state policy. The new direction was to change from an educational inputs policy to an educational outcomes policy, from a procedural accountability policy to an educational accountability policy, and

from a supplemental compensatory education for all policy to a high quality education for all policy (Webb, 2006, p. 334).

President Clinton appointed Richard Riley as his secretary of education. Secretary Riley became the longest serving secretary of education as he pushed to increase funding for Head Start and other programs meant to establish equality of educational opportunity. The idea was to reduce competition in which only the dominant culture could compete in order to level the playing field for all Americans. Linked to Clinton's agenda for equality of opportunity was his support for career training, school-to-work initiatives, and welfare reform programs which attempted to provide equality of economic opportunity as a natural result of equality of educational opportunity. Although he was able to hold off reductions in spending by a Republican Congress, he could neither increase spending to the degree he wanted to nor could he get all of his programs passed. He took criticism from conservative groups that thought his curriculum proposals lacked rigor and that emphasis on women and minorities was lowering the quality of the curriculum. In addition, religious groups opposed his programs.

A proponent of public school choice, Clinton had a major impact on public choice programs, in particular the most notable Milwaukee Parental Choice Program. He supported **open enrollment** which allowed families to choose from among public schools. To liberals, choice meant to allow students to attend smaller schools with smaller bureaucracies that would facilitate better teaching and better learning. Liberals also thought that choice programs could provide options for low-income students to attend better quality schools. Furthermore, this support of choice expanded into many different types of school models such as charter schools, **privatized schools**, **for-profit schools**, and others. By the end of the Clinton administration, legislation was passing which allowed different types of schools to advance the ideas of both public and private school

Open enrollment

An educational concept in the 1990s to allow families to choose which public schools their children should attend

Privatized schools

Schools run by private corporations

Profit schools

Schools run by private industry

choice. These laws led to a vast proliferation of varied schools throughout the rest of the 1990s and post-2000. These schools would serve minority, low-income, and religious populations as they grew in number. They were meant to provide additional opportunities for all Americans to succeed, even those in dominated cultures.

Also of note at this time were a number of court cases meant to end desegregation mandates for public schooling. *Board of Education of Oklahoma City v. McDowell* (1991) and *Freeman v. Pitts* (1992) determined that schools which have tried desegregation can then discontinue their efforts. Another case, *Missouri v. Jenkins* (1995) set a limit on school desegregation plans. Desegregation court cases such as these began the transition to the concept of resegregation that became evident after 2000 (Webb, 2006, pp. 334–345).

President George W. Bush: 2001–2009

Described as the greatest intrusion into local control of American education in the history of the federal government (Spring, 2002, p. 11), the Bush administration sought government control through massive legislation of educational mandates. These mandates meant that local schools spent most of their time and resources meeting state requirements as determined by federal law. Elected in 2000, President George W. Bush delivered an agenda which mirrored those of Presidents Reagan and George H. W. Bush. It emphasized private school vouchers, tuition tax credits, prayer in public schools, and reduced federal spending on education with increased spending on tests. Conservatives embraced the agenda. The biggest piece of legislation coming from the Bush administration was the huge No Child Left Behind Act.

The No Child Left Behind Act was passed in 2001 and enacted standardized testing on a massive scale and neutralized gains made since the 1960s toward creating a multicultural society through diversity education in the schools. The No Child Left

Behind Act mandated standardized tests and state standards to regulate the curriculum in order to produce high test scores. The No Child Left Behind Act, which required that all students take national tests administered by the National Assessment of Educational Progress, essentially created a **national school system with a national school curriculum.** Schools across the nation arranged their curricula to accommodate teaching that would prepare students for these mandated standardized tests. As of this writing, annual yearly progress is determined by test scores for each school within a district, and progress is determined by the percentage of students meeting proficiency in stated standards. If a school does not meet annual yearly progress levels, steps could be taken to punish the schools. In the extreme, these punishments have included school closings.

Critics of the No Child Left Behind Act state that the act reflects the history of American education because dominant culture populations in high performing schools perform better on standardized tests and thus meet annual yearly progress goals more effectively than dominated cultures in poor, underfunded schools. The critics say that standards and standardized tests without regard to the cultural framework of minority populations align themselves with the history of deculturalization and assimilation as has been evident in the evolution of American education. They claim that the No Child Left Behind Act is another 100% Americanization program. Underfunded, heavily minority populated schools are the schools failing the requirements and facing penalties. The children attending these schools have an unequal educational opportunity which leads to an unequal economic opportunity (Kozol, 2005, pp. 201–214). Supporters of the legislation state that this is the very reason why the law is a good one. The idea is to improve or close poorly performing schools so that all children can have equal educational opportunity which leads not only to personal fulfillment but to economic advantage for America

National school system with a national school curriculum

Federal mandates that began in 2001 are sometimes accused of creating this system because of mandatory national standards and testing

through the enhanced preparing of human capital. They claim that no child will be left behind in the quest for individual prosperity and national economic power (Webb, 2006, pp. 360–371).

President Bush continued the fight against bilingual education by failing to support the preservation of Native languages and by changing the name of the Office of Bilingual Education to the Office of English Language Acquisition. The Christian Coalition and many other similar groups around the nation have shown their support for his quest for an English-only dominant culture by not only electing him in 2000 but re-electing him in 2004. In this sense, President Bush symbolizes the continuance of the type of society that the ideological managers of the early eras in American history subscribed to. The policies he supports and passes assimilate minority cultures into the dominant culture. The gains made by minority populations over centuries are threatened by new legislation, and a return to the posturing of equal opportunity for the American population under a ruling class since the 1600s is evident in legislation symbolized by the Office of English Language Acquisition. The inclusion in the No Child Left Behind Act of a section entitled "Partnership in Character Education" is another example of President Bush's support from conservative groups. This section mandates character education in public school classrooms and includes the following examples as teaching units for character education:

- Caring
- Civic virtue and citizenship
- Justice and fairness
- Respect
- Responsibility
- Trustworthiness
- Giving

Since the passage of the No Child Left Behind Act, there has been debate over the secular or non-secular nature of these units as they are taught by local districts. This section of the No Child Left Behind Act

is reminiscent of the virtues so enforced by the Puritans, Noah Webster, and other early leaders of our nation.

Pressure on states to be responsible for education have continued to mount as the No Child Left Behind Act drains state resources, eliminates school programs, reduces teacher salary increases, and burdens local taxpayers. This financial burden creates massive program cutting emergencies on the parts of local school districts as they try to accommodate the No Child Left Behind Act. In addition, Christian fundamentalists see the law as an opportunity to push their agenda by initiating court cases to once again ask for prayer and Bible study in public schools. These groups see the President and the No Child Left Behind Act as permission to seek faith-based learning as seen in examples such as the 2002 Texas State Board of Education hearings at which scientific statements in textbooks banned the use of those textbooks as anti-technology, anti-Christian, and anti-American.

Immediately following the re-election of President Bush in 2004, state and local school boards began altering their policies regarding textbook content and curriculum offerings to challenge the secular nature of schools as had been the interpretation of the Constitution regarding separation of church and state. For example, the Texas State School Board forced a notable large textbook publishing company to change its secular definition of marriage to a non-secular definition. In Wisconsin, the Grantsburg Public School Board, led by its president who was a religious minister, passed a policy whereby evolution would not be the only theory of human origin taught in its public schools. The message was that creationism would now appear in its curriculum.

With many different paths to teacher certification now possible, President Bush in No Child Left Behind emphasized the need for highly qualified teachers. His administration finds that only 58% of English teachers, 47% of math teachers, 55% of science teachers, and 55% of social studies teachers are highly qualified. One stated definition of being

highly qualified is holding a teaching certificate in the subject one teaches. President Bush presses the states to create highly qualified teachers (Webb, 2006, pp. 367–369).

When President Bush was elected in 2000, there were 53.2 million K-12 students attending school. Within this population of students, the achievement gap between students of the dominant culture and students of dominated cultures was widening, according to many studies. This gap was not reduced by No Child Left Behind. In 2005 the Bush administration cut $12.7 billion from the federal student loan program. In 2006 the Bush administration proposed a cut of $5 billion in child support enforcement.

President Bush followed the pattern set by Ronald Reagan and mimicked by his father. He continued to escalate the push for tax credits, vouchers, and other incentives in favor of private and parochial schooling while he reduced federal funding and endorsements for programs for disadvantaged, low-income, and minority populations. He pushed for national standards and national testing based on dominant culture values. His opposition to bilingual education programs was a mark that set the tone for his agenda. More than ever since that time, it seems the American public and its leaders desire to create Jonathan Winthrop's republic of God-fearing, law-abiding citizens to create a single unified society.

Time Line of Civil Rights Events for Selected Ethnic Populations

1946–2005

Schools mirror society. In other words, the major trends and patterns that occur in society are mimicked in schools. On one level, when math becomes important in society, math becomes important in schools, or when phonics becomes important in society, phonics becomes important in schools. On a larger level, when the ideals of the majority ethnic population dominate society, then ethnic populations not in the majority struggle in their efforts to succeed in the general population. Because this has been the societal history of America, it is the same with schools. As schools have been dominated by the ideology of the dominant culture, cultures in the minority have struggled to succeed in the schools. The connection between schools and society is clear. Therefore, a *Time Line of Civil Rights Events for Selected Ethnic Populations* can be useful in paralleling the strides gained in schools as a result of the strides made in society. As the major trends and patterns in the general society influenced by the dominant culture made strides toward civil rights for minority populations, schools mirrored their progress as time unfolded. Though most of the events in the timeline below are not directly school events, they can be found embedded in patterns, trends, and, indeed, legislation that called for changes in school practice.

African Americans

1948
- President Harry S. Truman issues Executive Orders 9980 and 9981, which establish the President's Committee on Equality of Treatment and Opportunity in the Armed Services and the Fair Employment Board.

1950
- The NAACP Legal Defense Fund begins a campaign against the legality of the "separate but equal" concept.

1954
- The U.S. Supreme Court in *Brown v. Board of Education of Topeka, Kansas* decides that "separate" is inherently "unequal."
- The first White Citizens' Council is established in Indianola, Mississippi, to oppose desegregation and support White supremacy.

1955
- Rosa Parks is arrested in Montgomery, Alabama, for refusing to give up her bus seat.

- The Montgomery bus strike begins.
- Emmett Till is murdered.

1956

- Southern members of Congress sign the "Southern Manifesto" which condemns *Brown v. Board* as a violation of States' rights.
- The Montgomery Bus Boycott ends.

1957

- The Southern Christian Leadership Conference is established by Martin Luther King, Charles K. Steele, and Fred L. Shuttlesworth.
- The Little Rock Central High School desegregation demonstrations occur.

1960

- The Greensboro lunch counter sit-in occurs.
- The Student Nonviolent Coordinating Committee is founded.
- President John F. Kennedy issues Executive Order 10925, which mandates that projects financed with federal funds "take affirmative action" to ensure the hiring and employment practices are free of racial bias.

1961

- The Congress of Racial Equality begins sending "freedom riders" to Southern states to assist voter registration.

1962

- James Meredith enrolls at the University of Mississippi.

1963

- Martin Luther King is arrested and writes his "Letter from the Birmingham Jail."
- The Birmingham police brutality is televised around the nation.
- The March on Washington, DC, occurs.
- Denise McNair, Cynthia Wesley, Carole Robertson, and Addie May Collins are murdered at Sixteenth Street Baptist Church.

- President Kennedy stops Governor Wallace as he attempts to prohibit desegregation at the University of Alabama at Tuscaloosa.
- Martin Luther King wins the Nobel Peace Prize.
- Medgar Evers is murdered.

1964
- The 24th Amendment passes, abolishing poll taxes.
- The Council of Federated Organizations begins a large-scale effort to register Black voters during "Freedom Summer."
- President Lyndon Johnson signs the Civil Rights Act of 1964.
- James E. Chaney, Andrew Goodman, and Michael Schwerner are murdered by the Ku Klux Klan.

1965
- Malcolm X is murdered.
- The Pettus Bridge March results in Alabama's "Bloody Sunday."
- The Voting Rights Act of 1965 is passed.
- The Watts race riots occur in Los Angeles, California.
- Executive Order 11246, which requires government contractors to take affirmative action toward prospective minority employees in all aspects of hiring and employment, is issued by President Johnson.
- Huey Newton and Bobby Seale form the Black Panthers.

1966
- Stokely Carmichael coins the phrase "Black Power."
- Black Power initiates a break from the philosophy of non-violent protest.

1967
- The U.S. Supreme Court rules in *Loving v. Virginia* that prohibiting interracial marriage is unconstitutional.
- The Newark and Detroit race riots occur.

1968
- Martin Luther King is murdered.
- President Johnson signs the Civil Rights Act of 1968.
- Robert F. Kennedy is murdered.
- Shirley Chisholm becomes the first African American woman elected to Congress.
- In *Green v. County School Board of New Kent County* (Virginia) the U.S. Supreme Court rules that "actual desegregation" of schools in the South is required, ruling out "freedom of choice plans" and requiring affirmative action to integrate schools.

1969
- In *Alexander v. Holmes County Board of Education* the U.S. Supreme Court rules that the time limit for desegregating schools is over and that henceforth all segregated schooling is unconstitutional.

1971
- In *Swann v. Mecklenburg* the U.S. Supreme Court upholds busing to facilitate integration.

1973
- The U.S. Supreme Court in *Keyes v. School District No. 1, Denver, Colorado* rules that the Denver public school system is an unlawful "dual system" and that a remedy is required.

1978
- In *Regents of University of California v. Bakke* the U.S. Supreme Court determines that affirmative action is acceptable, but strict quotas are not.

1983
- In *Bob Jones University v. The United States* the U.S. Supreme Court upholds the Internal Revenue Service rule denying tax exemption to private schools that practice racial discrimination.

1988
- Congress overrides President Ronald Reagan's veto of the Civil Rights Restoration Act, which

limits the remedies available to the federal government in applying anti-bias rules to private organizations receiving federal subsidies.

1990

- Affirmative action is met with a more conservative approach when in *Adarand Constructors v. Pena* the U.S. Supreme Court decides that henceforth affirmative action cases must show that they serve some "compelling government interest."

1991

- President George H. W. Bush signs the Civil Rights Act of 1991.

1992

- Race riots occur in Los Angeles after four White LAPD police officers are acquitted for beating Rodney King, an African American man. The beating had been videotaped, and a segment of the tape had been broadcast on numerous occasions suggesting police brutality.

1996

- California adopts Proposition 209, which eliminates nearly all state affirmative action programs.

2003

- The U.S. Supreme Court rules in *Grutter v. Bollinger* that race can be one of many factors used to determine college entrance.
- The U.S. Supreme Court rules in *Gratz v. Bollinger* that universities may not blindly give extra weight to race in the admission process.

2005

- Edgar Ray Killan is convicted of manslaughter in the deaths of James E. Chaney, Andrew Goodman, and Michael Schwerner.

American Indians

1961

- The National Youth Indian Council is organized to resurrect a sense of national pride among

Indian young people and to instill an activist message.

1964

- Survival of American Indians, a newly formed activist organization, stages "Fish-ins" to preserve off-reservation fishing rights.
- Five Sioux Indians perform the first landing at Alcatraz.

1966

- Senator George McGovern introduces a resolution to increase Indian self-determination.

1968

- Congress passes the Indian Civil Rights Act requiring states to obtain tribal consent prior to passing laws regarding Indian reservations.
- United Native Americans is founded to promote Indian self-determination.
- The American Indian Movement is founded for protection from police abuse and to create job training, housing, and education programs.
- The Cornwall International Bridge is blockaded by Mohawk Indians to protest the U. S. restriction of Indian movement between the countries.

1969

- Navajo Community College at Many Farms, Arizona, opens as the first tribally established, Indian-controlled community college.
- The San Francisco American Indian Center burns down.
- Two attempts to occupy Alcatraz are led by Richard Oakes.
- The nineteen-month occupation of Alcatraz begins.
- Dennis Banks, co-founder of the American Indian Movement, spends two weeks at Alcatraz.

1970

- President Richard Nixon ends the 1950s termination policies and announces "self-determination without termination."

- Twenty-two legislative proposals are introduced supporting Indian self-rule.
- Governor Ronald Reagan establishes a $50,000 planning grant to the Bay Area Native American Council for urban Indians.
- On Thanksgiving Day the American Indian Movement paints Plymouth Rock red and takes over the Mayflower replica.

1971

- Alaska Natives gain 44 million acres of land and $962.5 million as a result of the efforts of the Alaska Native Claims Movement.
- The Alcatraz occupation ends.
- The American Indian Movement stages a "counter-celebration" on the Fourth of July by occupying the Mount Rushmore National Monument.
- Deganawide-Quetzalcoatl University in Northern California opens.

1972

- Richard Oakes is murdered.
- The Trail of Broken Treaties occurs in Washington, DC, and the Bureau of Indian Affairs is occupied.
- The Indian Education Act is passed, authorizing funding for special bilingual and bicultural programs, materials, training, and counselors.

1973

- Wounded Knee II occurs with 1,200 people arrested and three people killed.

1975

- The Jumping Bull Ranch Shootout occurs, and two FBI agents are killed.
- Leonard Peltier is sentenced to two life terms for the Jumping Bull Ranch deaths.
- The Indian Self-Determination and Education Assistance Act is passed to promote American Indian involvement in federal services to Indian communities.

1976

- The First Annual "Un-Thanksgiving Day" occurs.

1977

- AIM leaders conduct an International Treaty Conference with the United Nations in Geneva, Switzerland.
- The passage of approximately 50 laws regarding tribal issues regarding water rights, land, and fishing rights begins.

1978

- President Jimmy Carter approves the Indian Child Welfare Act regarding the guardianship and adoption of Indian children.
- Laws regarding tribal rights continue to be passed, helping redefine Indian issues such as water rights, fishing rights, and land acquisition.
- The "Longest Walk" occurs from Alcatraz to Washington, DC, to symbolize forced removal from Indian homelands.
- The American Indian Religious Freedom Act is passed.
- The Tribally Controlled Community College Assistance Act is passed, providing federal funding for Indian colleges.

1979

- The Treaty Fishing Rights decision of the U.S. Supreme Court is completed, reaffirming existing treaties and allowing for Indians to use 50% of fish in traditional fishing areas.

1980

- The Supreme Court decides that the United States government owes the Lakota Sioux interest from a payment for the Black Hills.
- The Lakotas refuse Black Hills payment in hopes of reclaiming the Black Hills.

1981

- The six-year occupation of the Black Hills at Yellow Camp begins as the Lakotas seek to reclaim their land.

1982
- The Indian Mineral Development Act is passed to encourage Indian tribes to become self-sufficient via mining their lands.
- The U.S. Supreme Court rules in *Seminole Tribe v. Butterworth* that tribes have the right to create gambling enterprises on their land, even if the state prohibits gambling.

1983
- The Nuclear Waste Policy Act is passed, requiring tribes to know where proposed high-level radioactive waste or a spent nuclear fuel repository will be located.

1985
- The American Indian Movement creates a security camp near Big Mountain, Arizona, to resist forced re-location of the Dine elders.

1987
- The Supreme Court upholds *Seminole Tribe v. Butterworth* in *California v. Cabazon*.

1988
- The Indian Gaming Regulatory Act is passed, allowing gaming on Indian land but requiring tribal/state negotiations.

1989
- The National Museum of American Indian Act orders the Smithsonian Institute to return Native American remains to American Indian tribes.
- Congress authorizes the building of a national Native American museum.

1990
- The Native American Languages Act is passed, supporting Native languages to be used in schools and elsewhere.
- The Native American Graves Protection and Repatriation Act is passed to require all federally funded institutions to inventory their collections of Indian human remains and artifacts, to

make their lists available to American Indians, and to return remains.

- The Indian Arts and Crafts Act is passed to reduce foreign and counterfeit product competition and to stop deception in marketing practices.

1992

- Several cities around the nation experience American Indian protests of the celebration of the 500th year of the arrival of Christopher Columbus.

1994

- An amendment to the American Indian Religious Freedom Act entitled the Native American Free Exercise of Religion Act is passed, allowing the use of peyote in religious ceremonies.
- President William J. Clinton issues an Executive Memorandum to clarify a "government-to-government" working relationship with tribes.
- The "Walk for Justice" occurs as AIM leaders walk on Alcatraz Island to protest the unjust imprisonment of Leonard Peltier.

1996

- President Clinton declares every November to be National Indian Heritage Month.
- President Clinton issues an Executive Order on Tribal Colleges and Universities to continue support and development of tribal colleges into the twenty-first century.
- President Clinton issues an Executive Order on Indian Sacred Sites to reaffirm the American Indian Religious Freedom Act and protection of sacred sites.

1997

- Native American Public Communications is established to promote Native American television and radio programming.

1999

- In South Dakota, protests occur over the breaking of the Danklow Acts, which gave 200,000 acres of tribal lands to the state.

- President Clinton visits Pine Ridge Reservation for a "nation-to-nation" business meeting which results in an empowerment zone for home ownership and economic development.
- 2000 American Indians return to Alcatraz for the 30th anniversary of its occupation.

2000
- The Red Cloud Building at the Pine Ridge Reservation is occupied.
- The Sand Creek National Monument Act is passed to recognize the site of the Sand Creek Massacre of Indians by federal and state soldiers.

2002
- The U.S. District Court of Oregon rules that the Kennewick man be returned to five Indian tribes.

2004
- The National Museum of the American Indian opens in Washington, DC.

Asian Americans

1952
- The Walter-McCarran Immigration and Naturalization Act repeals the Asian Exclusion Act of 1924 and allows a small number of Asians to immigrate to the United States with right of citizenship.

1953
- The Refugee Relief Act is passed, allowing non-quota immigration visas to Chinese and eastern European refugees.

1956
- Alien landownership laws are repealed in California.
- Dalip Singh is elected to the California Congress.

1959
- A "Confession Program" is created (lasting eight years) for Chinese persons residing illegally in the United States to confess their guilt and disclose

the identities of all relatives and friends also residing illegally.

1962

- Daniel K. Inouye is elected Hawaiian U.S. Senator.
- Spark Matsunaga is elected to the Hawaiian Congress.

1964

- Patsy Takemoto Mink is elected to the Hawaiian Congress.

1965

- The Immigration Act of 1965 is passed, eliminating race, creed, and nationality as a basis for immigration and allowing admission of 20,000 immigrants per year.

1967

- The U.S. Supreme Court rules that all anti-miscegenation laws are unconstitutional.

1968

- The first School of Ethnic Studies is created at San Francisco State College.

1974

- *Lau v. Nichols* is passed, enforcing bilingual-bicultural instruction to non-English speaking students.

1977

- The U.S. Supreme Court rules on the Bakke Case, upholding race as an acceptable factor in remedying the effects of past discrimination.

1978

- The Japanese American Citizens League adopts a resolution calling for the U.S. Government to redress its incarceration of Japanese Americans during WW II.

1979

- Asian-Pacific American Heritage Week is officially recognized.

1980
- The Commission on Wartime Relocation and Evacuation of Civilians (Redress Commission) is established to determine if incorrect actions were taken in the internment of Japanese Americans during WW II.
- The Refugee Act of 1980 is passed, increasing the number of refugees to enter the United States.

1981
- The Asian American Legal Defense Fund files a suit to stop luxury housing development in New York's Chinatown.
- Recent Asian immigrants are threatened by the Ku Klux Klan in Texas and California.

1982
- Vincent Chin is murdered by White auto workers in Detroit.

1983
- The Redress Commission calls for an official apology and payment of $20,000 to each surviving former internee.

1986
- Californians United is established to counter the English-only movement.
- A Cambodian home is firebombed in Revere, Massachusetts.

1987
- Racist attacks in Jersey City on Indo-Americans result in one death.

1988
- The Civil Liberties Act is passed to enact the recommendations of the Redress Commission.
- The Asian Labor Resource Center and American labor organizations hold a conference in New York to discuss employment and discrimination.

Hispanic/Latino Americans

1946

- The U.S. Supreme Court in *Mendez et al. v. Westminster School District of Orange County* determines that Mexican Americans are not Indians and that school segregation is illegal in California.

1948

- The U.S. Supreme Court determines school segregation to be illegal in Texas in *Delgado v. Bastrop Independent School District.*

1954

- The U.S. Supreme Court decides in *Hernandez v. Texas* that Mexican-Americans are a separate class of people facing discrimination.

1962

- Under the leadership of Cesar Chavez Community Service Organization chapters become effective at addressing civil rights issues, especially voter registration, police brutality, and citizenship.
- The National Farm Workers Association is created by Cesar Chavez.

1967

- La Raza Unida is established to preserve the culture and rights of Mexican Americans.
- The Mexican American Legal Defense and Education Fund is established.

1968

- The East Los Angeles High School walkout for educational rights occurs.
- The Bilingual Education Act is passed to provide federal funds to support bilingual programs.

1969

- The Spiritual Plan of Aztlan to encourage Chicano nationalism and liberation is adopted by the First National Chicano Liberation Youth Conference.

1970
- The U.S. Supreme Court decides in *Cisneros v. Corpus Christi* that the 1954 Brown decision applies to desegregation of Mexican Americans.

1973
- The U.S. Supreme Court decides that school finance is not a constitutional issue, and, therefore, cases of financial equity are to be settled by the states.

1974
- *Lau v. Nichols* is passed, enforcing bilingual-bicultural instruction to non-English speaking students.

1983
- Senator S. I. Hayakawa organizes U.S. English.

Glossary

Alternative, Charter, Choice Schools—Contemporary off-shoots of magnet schools, these schools are a mixture of public and private schools that offer specialized programs as an alternative to public schools.

Baby Boom—The increased number of human births from 1944 to 1964.

Business Model—School reform established in the 1980s that focused on a top-down corporate formula for success with clear goals and high standards to arrive at a quality product.

Chicano Movement—A movement prominent from 1965 to 1975 to press for Chicano studies in colleges and universities.

Cold War—A period beginning after World War II during which Russia and the United States monitored each other's weapons and form of government.

For-Profit Schools—Schools run by private industry.

La Raza Unida—An organization established in 1967 to protect the rights of Mexican Americans and to preserve their language and culture.

Magnet Schools—Specialty schools within a district to offer alternative school programs to encourage voluntary integration.

Mexican American Legal Defense Fund—An organization established in 1967 to protect rights of students punished for their involvement in civil rights issues.

National School System with a National School Curriculum— Federal mandates beginning in 2001 are sometimes accused of creating these through mandatory national standards and mandatory standardized testing.

Open Enrollment—An educational concept promoted in the 1990s to allow families to choose which public schools they wanted to attend.

Pan Indian Movement/American Indian Movement— Organizations formed in the 1960s to preserve Indian rights.

Privatized Schools—Schools run by private corporations.

Space Race—The competition between Russia and America to lead the world in knowledge of technology by developing space programs.

U. S. English—Founded in 1983, this group had as its goals to end bilingual education and to establish English as the national language.

Review

1. Describe and explain political events of this era.
2. Define and explain the social events of this era.
3. Define and explain the economic events of this era.
4. Explain *Brown v. Board* in relation to *Plessy v. Ferguson* and subsequent legislation after Brown.
5. Explain the origins of the NDEA and the ESEA and identify what each provided for education.
6. Create a timeline of major civil rights events of this era.
7. Discuss two major bills, one in 1972 and one in 1975, passed for minority populations.
8. It is 1961 and you are a White person living in Maine who has a strong concern for civil rights in America. What will you do?
9. Describe President Carter's impact on education.
10. What political precedent did President Carter set?
11. What observable support for women did President Carter display?
12. Describe the platform of presidential candidate Reagan.
13. It is 1977, and you are a Republican public middle school teacher. For whom will you vote in the 1980 election and why?
14. Describe the agendas that President Reagan supported and opposed regarding education.
15. How does federal funding relate to local control?
16. Which level of power and control, local, state, or federal, gained the most power and control from 1980–1992?

17. Describe President George H. W. Bush's agenda.
18. It is 1987, and you have just been nominated by the Republican Party to run for president in 1988. What will be your platform?
19. Summarize President Clinton's education agenda.
20. Identify and describe some educational programs passed during this era.
21. President Clinton called for business partnerships with schools. What other eras had the same ideas?
22. What is the difference between public school choice and private school choice?
23. It is 1994, and you are a Democrat discussing politics with a Republican. Do you consider President Clinton to be a liberal or a conservative?
24. Summarize President George W. Bush's education agenda.
25. What other presidents had the same agendas as President George W. Bush?
26. Describe the No Child Left Behind Act.
27. What other presidents called for increased testing in public schools?
28. You are a student in a class in 2002. Your teacher asks you if you live in a liberal or a conservative society. What do you say? What do you give as evidence?
29. Explain how presidents impact education.
30. What thoughts do you have at this point regarding the evolution of American education?

Selected Topics for Further Study

1. Immigration Acts of 1924 and 1965
2. Multicultural education from 1944 to 1975
3. League of United Latin American Citizens (LULAC), MALDEF (Mexican American Legal Defense Education Fund), NAACP (National Association for the Advancement of Colored People)
4. American Indian Movement
5. The impact of the War on Poverty as seen in schools
6. The impact of the Vietnam War as seen in schools
7. Bilingual education
8. Federal legislation for the handicapped
9. Secretary Shirley M. Hufstedler
10. U.S. Department of Education
11. Minority employees in federal jobs, 1976–2008
12. Vouchers and tuition tax credits
13. Separation of church and state

14. Bilingual education research, programs, laws by states
15. Levels of federal, state, and local funding for education from 1980 to 1992
16. Civil rights events in modern American history
17. Federal, state, and local funding patterns from 1976 to 2005
18. The impact of No Child Left Behind on public, private, and parochial schools
19. Religious education laws passed from 2000 to 2008
20. Senator S. I. Hayakawa
21. Secretary of Education Rod Paige
22. Secretary of Education Margaret Spellings
23. The Milwaukee Parental Choice Program
24. Charter schools
25. For-profit schools
26. Equalization laws for school programming
27. Laws regarding religion in public schools
28. The effects of wars on education
29. Teaching patriotism in public schools
30. Education in a global society
31. through 42. Presidents and their educational efforts:
    Truman
    Eisenhower
    Kennedy
    Johnson
    Nixon
    Ford
    Carter
    Reagan
    Bush
    Clinton
    Bush

Where We Have Been and Where We Are Now

The evolution of American education has taken place since the founding of our nation in the 1600s. Jonathan Winthrop and his band of followers sought to avoid religious persecution in England. They began to set up communities in the New England area that were meant to be the models for what would eventually become American society. Eventually many factors came into play as education unfolded throughout the centuries. Five philosophical, religious, social, economic, and political factors stand out. The evolution of American education can be viewed through the development of these generalized primary factors. As these primary factors identified the focus at any time or during any period, they were accompanied by individuals and groups that controlled how these factors influenced education. These individuals and groups came to be known as the ideological managers of the evolution of American education. It is through the struggle of differing individuals and groups that we come to see which

ideological managers prevailed during each era to determine the direction of education.

1636–1723

American schools began as instruments of religion. Under the Protestant theology carried over from Europe, very early schools began to develop in the wilderness of our country. The ideological managers of this era sought to create moral, God-fearing citizens. Religious indoctrination and social norm factors joined to promote politically motivated acts in 1642 and 1647 that developed schooling along the lines of Protestant theology. These two acts, the Massachusetts Law of 1642 and the Deluder Satan Act of 1647, became the first major educational laws. The first schools were created as reading and writing schools for non-college-bound, non-leadership-bound students. Latin/grammar schools were created for college-bound (Harvard, 1636) and leadership-bound (politicians) students. For those heading for specific trades, apprenticeship schools were created. All schools were based on the religious belief in reading the Bible and writing out scriptures in order to lead a moral, God-fearing (and thus virtuous) life. The Calvinist philosophy prevailed.

1723–1830

This era brought about dramatic change as some leaders of the country challenged the prevailing ideological managers. The Intellectual Revolution was spawned by *Cato's Letters* and brought to the fore later by Thomas Jefferson. Jefferson challenged the notion that education should only be rote memorization of the Bible to nurture obedient servers to God, country, and father. Jefferson and his followers wanted more freedoms, specifically the freedoms of thought, speech, and the press. They accepted the religious, philosophical, social, and political beliefs that had been driving the early ideological managers but wanted to broaden them to include not only the already established moral, God-fearing education but also what was called education for virtue for future leadership. This idea combined the rigidity of order with the quest for more freedoms and resulted in the balance of freedom and order argument primarily engaged by Jefferson and Noah Webster. A compromise based primarily on political factors was reached: Jefferson and Webster agreed that more freedoms could be incorporated as long as there was the focus on education for virtue. This ideological compromise basically meant that education could result in a broader range of learning experience, but that it was still meant to create virtuous citizens to serve the nation in moral, God-fearing ways and, it could be added, dominant culture ways. Schools continued to be philosophically Calvinistic but became more open to education beyond rote memorization of the Bible. For example, academies were developed to teach both ornamental (status) knowledge and utilitarian (useful) knowledge. Ben Franklin's Academy was the most famous model, even though it was never physically built. These schools surpassed the reading and writing schools, Latin/grammar schools, and apprenticeship schools and went on to include not only religious, social, and political orientation but also preparation for work/jobs/employment. Also at this time hierarchies of control began to develop regarding the organization and control of schools. One of the popular leaders emerging along these lines was Joseph Lancaster who introduced a monitorial system. What was once a struggling republic had now become a nation; therefore, society and schools experienced an even greater push toward nationalism. This trend escalated.

1830–1895

This era found the ideological managers of the dominant culture fighting to maintain their control on many fronts. A new country had emerged, and unification became a major issue. The leaders in society pushed for unification through a common school ideology. Thus, the common school movement dominated education in this era. The goals of the common school movement, most notably professed by Horace

Mann, were to educate all school-going children in a common school with a common social/political curriculum. It was at this time that schools were first recognized as the official purveyors of the government's will. The key to creating a good society was using the schools to do so. The Calvinistic philosophy was not totally abandoned, but a new philosophy, based on the blank slate concept, was adopted. This philosophy, taken from John Locke, allowed the schools to determine that children know little to nothing and can be socially and politically indoctrinated if schools and teachers write out the government's curriculum on their blank slates (minds). This highly nationalistic curriculum fostered the unification that the ideological managers desired. The entire school experience was set up to promote the values of the Anglo-Saxon, Protestant, White, wealthy male: the dominant culture. Common school devices such as the use of only nationalistic literature, the use of Webster's English dictionary and speller, the use of McGuffey's readers, and the use of other dominant culture literature were combined with the use of patriotic songs, dances, anthems, and allegiances to promote national unity based on the dominant culture's value structure.

This era's innovations exerted an enduring impact on American schools, most notably the identification and recruitment of women as ideal teachers. Teacher institutes and normal schools were established to train teachers not only in pedagogy but also in bringing up America's students to be moral and virtuous. Johann Pestalozzi, Friedrich Froebel, and Jean-Jacques Rousseau all contributed to the ideas of republican motherhood and the maternal model of instruction. Women were thought to be ideal nurturers and teachers, and children were seen as having huge potential. Juxtaposed to this maternal model was the widespread use of the Joseph Lancaster driven monitorial system of school management, a rigid, religion-based, authoritarian method of teaching in schools that led to indoctrination for national unity and a strict adherence to obedience.

Native Americans had been treated as heathens and savages since the early 1600s. Leaders, including Washington, Jefferson, and John Adams, had been attempting to eliminate Native Americans for 200 years via a variety of different plans to take their land and deculturalize them. The usual techniques of deculturalization, taking away language, traditions, and education, came to a head during this era with the Indian Removal Act and the Trail of Tears, which were justified by several federal court decisions. The Native Americans were removed, slaughtered, and pushed aside until the 1950s when they began to regain some of their rights.

Other dominated cultures suffered the same fate as the Native Americans. African Americans, who had to fight to move from a total absence of schooling to inferior, segregated education, continued to struggle against domination in this era. Southern Blacks established oral traditions of song and dance while Northern Blacks attempted political challenges for the rights to be free and educated. In both cases, efforts were futile as African Americans were simply looked upon as slaves for White people (or **servants** after the official abolition of slavery). It would take another generation for significant change to begin to occur for African Americans.

Servants

The newer or modern term for slaves after 1863 and the abolition of slavery

Asian populations and Mexican populations suffered the same fate as Native Americans and African Americans under the White dominant culture and determined minority deculturalization techniques. The fear of the "yellow peril," of the idea that Asian Americans were taking White people's jobs, motivated the usual deculturalization techniques on Asian Americans. "Keeping them on their knees" was one of the concepts that explained Mexican Americans being coerced out of schools and into the fields to do the manual labor for wealthier White farmers. Asian Americans and Mexican Americans, like Native Americans and African Americans, had to overcome social, political, religious, economic, and philosophical discrimination to arrive at any education for their children, much less equal education. Suffice it

to say, education was not equal during the time of the common school movement as the wealthier White dominant culture solidified its ideas for national unity. It would take Asian Americans and Mexican Americans another hundred years to begin realizing substantial gains.

One population that did make significant strides during the common school movement was the population of Irish Catholics. Feeling the weight of the Anglo-Saxon, Protestant-oriented school curriculum and the resulting disfranchisement of their children, the Irish Catholics established what is now known as the parochial school system via the Plenary Councils. After social, political, and economic upheaval that in some cases led to violence, the Irish Catholics split from the common school movement and created their own schools.

Thus, the common school movement never became what it was intended to be: a common school for all. It never achieved its goal of an education for all people of all social, economic, political, and religious classes.

1895–1920

This era started with a bang as Booker T. Washington made his famous speech in Atlanta. Since the end of the Civil War and Reconstruction, America had been transitioning from an agrarian to an industrial society. This change led to a need for more factory workers. Washington told industrial leaders to look no further; they should allow schools to train African Americans to work in the factories. His speech set off a new commitment to segregated schools as *Plessy v. Ferguson* passed the so-called "separate but equal" federal law. These two events escalated the argument over the education of dominated versus dominating populations. W. E. B. Du Bois entered the argument as a proponent of not only educational equality but also social equality. Although his goal was to achieve social equality via educational and economic opportunity, this effort put off his demands for over 50 years until *Brown v. Board* was passed.

As African American educational, economic, and social opportunities and rights remained in check during this era, other dominated populations experienced the same plight. In America, the dominant culture still prevailed, but inroads were beginning to plant ideas for future, larger gains for dominated populations. Although slow and small, segregated schools began their steps toward equalized education. The industrial revolution with its need for more workers seemed to fuel this hope for desegregation and equal rights both in school and in society for future generations.

Schools responded to the industrial revolution, increased urbanization, and another wave of immigrants by developing factory model schools but with an eye to national unity. Vocational education received a major boost and became a focus of education. Frederick Taylor's factory model for schools was designed to teach punctuality, work habits, and, most of all, standardization of procedures for the most efficient outcome. This emphasis on responding to the industrial revolution, urbanization, and immigration led to the next school movement. The comprehensive school movement's key descriptor was its differentiated curriculum which began what is now known as tracking. Students were (and still are) tracked into college bound, general, or vocational education tracks in order to sort and train individuals in specific areas for specific occupations to serve as human capital to catapult America into a global economic leadership role. Therefore, educational, social, political, philosophical factors were controlled to develop economic power.

In addition, schools of this era continued their mission to serve the government's will by escalating their attempts to foster national unity via the dominant culture. As school attendance skyrocketed in this time of great change, a plethora of 100% Americanization programs developed to promote the common values of the dominant culture.

The 1920s, the 1930s, and the 1940s

Social, political, and economic factors dominated the ideological management of this era. As a result, the comprehensive school movement realized its full force as a factory model of vocational education designed to generate human capital to establish America as a global economic power. At the same time, the comprehensive school movement featured an increase in 100% Americanization programs which put national unity via its dominant culture at the top of everyone's school agenda. This eventuated the growth of schools as social centers so that they could shape society in the (dominant culture) American way. Playgrounds, sandlots, auditoriums, organized sports, school assemblies, student senate, and school newspapers were some of the major arenas more fully developed by schools to indoctrinate students in 100% Americanization. Social efficiency became a watch phrase to hitch on to the previous Lancasterian model of *let there be no idle moments* and Taylor's standardization for production ideas. John Dewey and his followers came on the scene to argue that education should be a process of living in and of itself, not a preparation for future living. Dewey wanted much more than only vocational education.

Major social factors came into play during this era. The aftermath of World War I, unions gaining power, the suffragettes, prohibition, the Jazz Age, the Depression, and the coming of World War II all played major roles in school and society. These developments led to the creation of such programs as the NYA (National Youth Administration), the CCC (Civilian Conservation Corps), and the WPA (Works Progress Administration).

The era ended with 100% Americanization comprehensive schools in full force featuring a differentiated curriculum, an increased testing, and an emphasis in vocational education. By this time, however, the formation of such groups as the NAACP (National Association for the Advancement of Colored People) and LULAC (League of United Latin American

Citizens) brought about renewed efforts to end deculturalization and foster equality. These organizations began pursuing the rights of the dominated cultures with some success.

1944–1975

The years immediately following World War II found a booming economy and a society on the move. High hopes for America as an economic and political leader abounded. Along with these high hopes came high hopes for and a renewed interest in education. While economic factors were in high gear and going well, the U.S.S.R. and its **Communist Block** were threatening to establish themselves as the world's political leaders. Another Red Scare occurred, and as Americans began to worry about a Communist takeover, schools came under fire. Called the weakest link in the fight against Communism by people such as Art Bestor and Hyman Rickover, schools were deemed anti-intellectual. Critics demanded curriculum change with a back-to-basics focus. To a large degree this demand was met in 1957 after *Sputnik* went up and when in 1958 the National Defense Education Act was passed. This act provided major federal funding for math, science, and foreign languages to produce a defense in human capital against Communist advances in technology that could be used to defeat America. As baby boomers began attending schools in large numbers, the concept of large schools with a differentiated curriculum to sort and train for human capital now included a large emphasis on math, science, and foreign languages.

As the nation dealt with its Communist scare, it also dealt with renewed civil rights efforts by dominated cultures that were met with firm resistance by the dominant culture. In 1955 Rosa Parks's decisive action of sitting in the front of a bus sparked the city-wide public transit strike in Montgomery, Alabama. In 1957 Governor Faubus caused a confrontation in Little Rock when he attempted to ban Black students from attending the local public school. The

Communist Block

The countries of the world aligned with the Soviet Union during the Cold War years

lunch counter eruption, freedom riders, murders, lynchings, and a plethora of events reflected the continuing racial strife in America. In 1963 Martin Luther King made one of his most memorable marches and his most memorable speech in Washington, DC. In 1967 MALDEF (Mexican American Legal Defense Education Fund) and La Raza Unida were created to attempt to uphold civil rights in courts of law. In 1969 Native Americans took over what used to be Alcatraz prison in the San Francisco Bay to symbolize their desire for a return of their culture. Not at first, but slowly and over time, these efforts began to make a difference in the struggle for civil rights. It started with *Brown v. Board* in 1954 and the 1955 Enforcement Decree and continued with the 1964 Civil Rights Act and such laws as the Bilingual Education Act of 1968, *Cisneros v. Corpus Christie Independent School District* (1970), Indian Education Act of 1972, and the Indian Self-Determination Act of 1975. The 1960s came to be recognized as a time of change which brought about more multicultural schools in an increasingly diversified society.

It cannot be ignored that during this same era the Red Scare was fueled by the Korean War and later the war in Vietnam. By the time the war in Vietnam escalated, liberals in the country began protesting the war. Large-scale demonstrations and civil unrest erupted. The demonstrations became violent, and strong feelings on both sides of the issue permeated society. The Kent State tragedy on May 4, 1970, marked the end of violent protests against the war, and President Nixon, elected in 1968, assumed the leadership of restoring order in a conservative response to the liberal 1960s. Schools once again were asked to take a back-to-basics approach with an emphasis on a core curriculum of math and science. Added to this curriculum was a substantial component of business/school partnership education, accountability on the parts of teachers and students, and the initiation of large-scale test-based documentation of achievement. Magnet schools and alternative schools were

developed as attempts to achieve integration.

Also in this era, President Lyndon Johnson established his War on Poverty which took America in a new direction. Poverty and discrimination were believed to deter the development of human capital, reducing America's capacity to remain a world economic and political leader. To fight this problem, Johnson passed the Elementary and Secondary Education Act which created massive funding for programs, including Head Start and others, that were intended to create an equal educational opportunity for all.

The women's movement of the 1960s and 1970s led to the passage of the Higher Education Act of 1972. This act provided for gender equality both in employment and in education. These provisions applied to all schools, pre-kindergarten to graduate, public and private. Although *Grove City College v. Bell* restricted Title IX to specific education programs in 1983, it was overturned in 1987 by the Civil Rights Restoration Act, which covered all activities of any institution receiving federal aid.

Continuing the work of the 1960s for equal civil and educational rights for the handicapped, the Pennsylvania Association for Retarded Children (PARC) played a part in the passage of the monumental PL 94–142 (1975). This bill was entitled the Education for All Handicapped Children Act and resulted in the requirement of the Individual Educational Plan (IEP).

1975–2008

President Carter set the standard for connecting presidential politics with education by striking his deal with the National Education Association to establish the United States Office of Education as a separate and distinct entity to promote American education. Though public schools stood to gain from President Carter's association with pro-public education groups, the expected large increases in federal funding and legislation did not occur. Much of this lack of progress reflected domestic economic problems and a plethora

Religious right
A plethora of organizations and individuals who espouse to and promote conservative religious values

of foreign policy issues.

In the 1980 and 1984 elections, Americans voted with the **religious right** and the conservative sector of the nation. The two terms of the conservative President Reagan resulted in a reduction in funding and legislation for public schools while private and parochial schools experienced benefits through vouchers, tuition tax credits, and religion in public schools. In 1983, the government-generated report *A Nation at Risk* blamed schools for the United States not keeping up in the world economic market. It called for yet another effort to install an intense back-to-basics curriculum while opening doors for more choice, charter, and alternative schools to develop. Another report entitled *Action for Excellence* called once again for a closer relationship between schools and business. Both of these reports resulted in increased pressure for programs at the local level after President Reagan had cut federal funding. When President George H. W. Bush was elected in 1988, he continued the themes of the previous eight years.

In a conservative society under conservative leadership, dominated populations found it difficult to continue making gains in civil and personal rights. The most prominent example of diminished capacity for dominated cultures was seen in the anti-bilingual efforts espoused by the conservatives of this era. In 1983 an organization called U.S. English was created to promote a single national language. Secretary of Education William Bennett appointed presidential advisory committee members who supported anti-bilingual efforts, leading President Reagan to be accused of an unholy alliance with right-wing groups. Further gains came slowly if at all for dominated cultures.

President Clinton, elected in 1992, tried to reverse the trend away from public school support by increasing federal funding for public education and revitalizing public opinion regarding public education. A strong proponent of the link between school and work, Clinton passed the Goals 2000 Educate America

Act in 1994. This act increased federal funding for pre-school and adult learning and also Head Start. Clinton also passed the School-to-Work Opportunities Act, which granted federal funds for schools with both school-based and work-based programs for education and employment. To support higher expectations for teacher standards, President Clinton established the National Board of Professional Teaching Standards. A pro-public school choice advocate, Clinton supported programs such as the Milwaukee Parental Choice Program. Many other different types of schools were created as well such as non-profit, for-profit, and business venture schools. The national emphasis on career education as well as Clinton's desire to include women's studies and multicultural education led to criticism from conservatives on the grounds that these ideas lacked rigor. In the end, President Clinton was unable to fund education as fully as he wanted or to pass all the pro-education legislation he supported.

President George W. Bush, elected in 2000, will leave the monumental federal legislation entitled No Child Left Behind as his educational legacy. This act mandates testing to levels never before seen throughout American educational history. Schools must demonstrate annual yearly progress toward standards based on student test results or face punishments, including closing the respective school. The central theme of the legislation is to hold schools accountable for student learning through diligent testing against sets of standards that increase competition among and between schools. Competition is the vehicle through which schools are to improve. Re-elected in 2004 by conservatives who support his standards and test movements, President Bush has continued to press the No Child Left Behind Act. He has also pushed for increased private school funding and legislation supporting increases in private charter and voucher schools, some publicly funded. The emphasis on local control results in local public schools taking on increased requirements from state agencies to meet federal guidelines under No Child

Left Behind. Liberals argue that the No Child Left Behind Act is reducing critical thinking in school curricula in the quest to meet mandated test score increases. They also contend that dominated groups are shortchanged by assessments created in the norms of the dominant culture. Liberals fear increased oppression of the dominated cultures while conservatives claim schools will improve for all by holding them accountable. Public school advocates claim the Bush presidency aims to end public schooling by influencing parents to send their children to private schools and by pushing for the closing of public schools, rather than working to improve public schools.

The anti-bilingualism of the 1980s has been re-established as the Office of English Acquisition, which serves as a guide for English-only advocates. Conservatives who support anti-bilingualism also support President Bush's Partnership in Education, which mandates character education in public schools. This character education is supported by religious groups attempting to increase the role of religion in public schools.

The evolution of American educational history is a fascinating reflection of who we have been and what we are in America. It reveals the complex and multifaceted development of our society and thus our schools. By studying the major players as ideological managers in the struggle for power and control in American society, we can see that the pendulum swings back and forth in cycles from conservative to liberal views. Within these views, social, political, philosophical, economic, and religious factors play out to develop what we see as American public schools.

For now, America is in its conservative cycle of ideological management of what occurs in schools. A back-to-basics curriculum with a focus on science and math is the current push in American education. Along with continued emphasis on school and business partnerships for employment education to help

manage human capital which will keep America as a world economic and political power, this is the thrust of contemporary education. Conservatives are mandating national unity through standards and standardized testing. Public schools are being held accountable for achieving test results to prove annual yearly progress while various private schools are proliferating. Court cases promoting religion in public schools abound across the states. The society's predominant culture agenda leaves little to no room for any dominated culture or **oppressed population**. How long will these themes make up the ideological management of education in America? Will dominated groups have any chance in the future for equal educational/economic opportunity? Will new ideological managers arise in the future and, if so, what will their agendas be? What does the future hold in the evolution of American education?

Oppressed population

Any number of different individuals or groups whose ideas, circumstances, or lifestyles are suppressed by a dominant culture

Glossary

Communist Block—The countries of the world aligned with the Soviet Union during the Cold War years.

Oppressed Population—Any variety of individuals or groups whose ideas, circumstances, or lifestyles are suppressed by a dominant culture or by any other from of oppression.

Religious Right—A plethora of organizations and individuals who espouse to and promote conservative religious values for mainstream America.

Servants—The newer or modern term for slaves after 1863 and the abolition of slavery.

Review

1. What is your reaction to this overview of the evolution of American education?
2. Are your emotional and intellectual reactions different? How?
3. Has this overview inspired critical thinking about educational issues in the past and present?
4. What specific connections do you see through time in each of the primary factors discussed?
5. What educational movements or trends could be traced from the seed of their beginnings to their presence in time

in educational policy to their waning of popularity as time evolved?

6. What generalized statements and conclusions could you make regarding the evolution of American education?

7. On what trends or movements will education evolve into the future?

8. Who will be the educational ideological managers of the future?

9. What will schools look like in 50, 100, 150 years?

10. What did you learn from this text?

Selected Topics for Further Study

1. The office of the presidency and its impact on American education

2. Political trends of the next 50 years and their impacts on American education

3. Social trends of the next 50 years and their impacts on American education

4. Economic trends of the next 50 years and their impacts on American education

5. Religious trends of the next 50 years and their impacts on American education

6. Technological trends of the next 50 years and their impacts on American education

7. Population shifts of the next 50 years and their impacts on American education

8. Global education and the changing nature of American schools in response to global education

9. American education in 2060: What will it look like?

10. American education in 2100: What will it be?

References

Banks, J. A., & McGee Banks, C. A. (1997). *Multicultural education: Issues and perspectives* (3rd ed.). Needham Heights, MA: Allyn & Bacon.

Bourne, P. G. (1997). *Jimmy Carter: A comprehensive biography from Plains to post-presidency.* New York: Scribner.

Counts, G. S. (1932). *Dare the schools build a new social order?* Carbondale, IL: Southern Illinois University.

Demos, J. (1970). *A little commonwealth: Family life in Plymouth Colony.* New York: Oxford University Press.

Dewey, J. (1997). *Experience and education.* New York: Touchstone. (Original work published 1938)

Du Bois, W. E. B. (1903). *The souls of black folk: Essays and sketches.* Chicago.

Giddings, P. (1984). *When and where I enter: The impact of black women on race and sex in America.* New York: Perennial.

Grant, C., & Sleeter, C. E. (1986). *After the school bell rings.* Philadelphia: Falmer.

Hlebowitsh, P. S. (2001). *Foundations of American education* (2nd ed.). Belmont, CA: Wadsworth/Thomson.

Johnson, D. W., & Johnson, F. P. (1997). *Joining together: Grouping therapy and grouping schools.* Boston: Allyn Bacon.

Johnson, T. W. (2002). *Historical documents in American education.* Boston: Allyn & Bacon.

Kaestle, C. F. (1983). *The pillar of the republic: Common schools and American society, 1780–1860.* New York: Hill and Wang.

Katz, M. B. (1987). *Reconstructing American education.* Cambridge, MA: Harvard University Press.

Mondale, S., & Patton, S. B. (Eds.). (2001). *School: The story of American public education.* Boston: Beacon.

Murphy, M. M. (2006). *The history and philosophy of education: Voices of educational pioneers.* Upper Saddle River, NJ: Pearson.

Nash, M. A. (2005). *Women's education in the United States: 1780–1840.* New York: Palgrave McMillan.

National Commission on Excellence in Education. (1984). *A nation at risk: The full account.* Cambridge, MA: USA Research.

Reese, W. J. (2005). *America's public schools: From the common school to "No Child Left Behind."* Baltimore: Johns Hopkins University Press.

Schuman, D. (2004). *American schools, American teachers: Issues and perspectives.* Boston: Pearson.

Spring, J. (2001a). *The American school: 1642–2000* (5th ed.). Boston: McGraw-Hill.

Spring, J. (2001b). *Deculturilization and the struggle for equality.* New York: McGraw-Hill.

Spring, J. (2002). *Conflict of interest: The politics of American education* (4th ed.). New York: McGraw-Hill.

Washington, B. T. (1901). *Up from slavery.* Garden City, NY: Doubleday and Company.

Webb, D. L. (2006). *The history of American education: A great American experiment.* Upper Saddle River, NJ: Pearson.

Wesely, C. H. (1984). *The history of the National Association of Colored Women's Clubs, Inc.: A legacy of service.* Washington, DC: National Association of Colored Women's Clubs.

Further Readings

Books

Ambrose, S. E. (1990). *Eisenhower: Soldier and president.* New York: Touchstone.

Ambrose, S. E. (2000). *Nothing like it in the world: The men who built the transcontinental railroad 1863–69.* New York: Simon & Schuster.

Anderson, J. D. (1988). *The education of blacks in the south, 1960–1935.* Chapel Hill, NC: University of North Carolina Press.

Bracey, G. W. (2002). *The war against America's public schools: Privatizing schools, commercializing education.* Boston: Allyn & Bacon.

Brands, H. W. (2000). *The first American: The life and times of Benjamin Franklin.* New York: Anchor Books.

Brock, D. (2002). *Blinded by the right: The conscience of an ex-conservative.* New York: Three Rivers Press.

Cremin, L. A. (1951). *The American common school.* New York: Columbia.

Cubberly, E. P. (1919). *Public education in the United States.* Boston: Houghton-Mifflin.

Cunningham, N. E., Jr. (1987). *In pursuit of reason: The life of Thomas Jefferson.* New York: Ballantine Books.

Dawly, A. (2000). *Class & community: The Industrial Revolution in Lynn.*Cambridge: Harvard University Press.

Dewey, J. (1933). *How we think: A restatement of the relation of reflective thinking to the education process.* New York: Houghton-Mifflin.

Diamond, J. (1999). *Guns, germs, and steel: The fates of human societies.* New York: W. W. Norton.

Ellis, J. J. (2000). *Founding brothers: The revolutionary generation.* New York: Alfred A. Knopf.

Erikson, E. H. (1950). *Childhood and society.* New York: W. W. Norton.

Fleming, T. (1999). *Duel: Alexander Hamilton, Aaron Burr and the future of America:* New York: Basic Books.

Franklin, J. H. (1976). *Racial equality in America.* Columbia: University of Missouri Press.

Franklin, J. H., & Meier, A. (Eds.). (1982). *Black leaders of the twentieth century.* Chicago: University of Illinois Press.

Friedan, B. (1962). *The feminine mystique.* New York: Sell.

Goldston, R. (1968). *The great Depression: The United States in the thirties.* Greenwich, CT: Fawcett.

Gonzalez, G. (1990). *Chicano education in the era of segregation.* Philadelphia: Balch Institute.

Halberstam, D. (1993). *The fifties.* New York: Villard.

Hastings, M. (1987). *The Korean War.* New York: Simon & Schuster.

Hendrickson, P. (2003). *Sons of Mississippi: A story of race and its legacy.* New York: Random House.

Koning, H. (1976). *Columbus: His enterprise. Exploding the myth.* New York: Monthly Review.

Kozol, J. (2006). *The shame of the nation: The restoration of apartheid schooling in America.* New York: Crown.

McCall, N. (1997). *What's going on?* New York: Vintage Books.

McCourt, F. (1996). *Angela's ashes.* New York: Touchstone.

McCourt, F. (1999). *'Tis: a memoir.* New York: Scribner.

Moore, J. M. (2003). *Booker T. Washington, W. E. B. Du Bois, and the struggle for racial uplift.* Wilmington, DE: Scholarly Resources.

Moore, M. (2001). *Stupid white men.* New York: Harper Collins.

Naisbitt, J. (1982). *Megatrends: Ten new directions transforming our lives.* New York: Warner.

Nye, J. S., Jr. (2002). *The paradox of American power: Why the world's only super power can't go it alone.* New York: Oxford.

Postman, N., & Weingartner, C. (1989). *Teaching as a subversive activity.* New York: Delacorte.

Pulliam, J. D., & Van Patten, J. J. (2007). *History of education in America.* Upper Saddle River, NJ: Pearson.

Randall, W. S. (1990). *Benedict Arnold: Patriot and traitor.* New York: William Morrow.

Ravitch, D. (2000). *Left back: A century of failed school reforms.* New York: Simon & Schuster.

Reeves, R. (2001). *President Nixon: Alone in the White House.* New York: Simon & Schuster.

Ryan, A. (1995). *John Dewey and the high tide of American liberalism.* New York: W. W. Norton.

Schlesinger, A. M., Jr. (2002). *A thousand days: John F. Kennedy in the White House.* New York: Houghton Mifflin.

Schlosser, E. (2001). *Fast food nation.* New York: Perennial.

Smith, P. (1984). *The rise of industrial America: A people's history of the Post-Reconstruction era.* New York: McGraw-Hill.

Stowe, H. B. (1966). *Uncle Tom's cabin.* New York: Penguin.

Tanenhaus, S. (1997). *Whittaker Chambers.* New York: Random House.

Thomas, H. (1999). *Front row at the White House: My life and time.* New York: Schribner.

Toffler, A. (1920). *Future shock.* New York: Random House.

Tyack, D. B., & Cuban, L. (1995). *Tinkering toward utopia: A century of public school reform.* Cambridge, MA: Harvard University Press.

Watkins, W. H., Lewis, J. H., & Chou, V. (2001). *Race and education: The roles of history and society in educating African American students.* Needham Heights, MA: Allyn & Bacon.

Weatherford, J. (1988). *Indian givers: How Indians of the Americas transformed the world.* New York: Fawcett Columbine.

Zubok, V., & Pleshakou, C. (1996). *Inside the Kremlin's Cold War: From Stalin to Khrushchev.* Cambridge: Harvard.

Articles

Baker, D. P., & Riordan, C. (1998). The 'eliting' of the common American Catholic school and the national education crises. *Phi Delta Kappan, 80*(1), 16–23.

Beane, J. A. (1998). Reclaiming a democratic purpose for education. *Educational Leadership, 56*(2), 8–11.

Bomotti, S. (1998). Pondering the complexities of school choice. *Phi Delta Kappan, 80*(4), 313–317.

Borman, G. D. (2002/2003). How can Title 1 improve achievement? *Educational Leadership, 60*(4), 49–53.

Boyd, W. L., & Nathan, J. (2003). Lessons about school choice from Minnesota: Promise and challenge. *Phi Delta Kappan, 84*(5), 350–355.

Bracey, G. W. (1998). The eighth Bracey report on the condition of public education. *Phi Delta Kappan, 80*(2), 112–131.

Clinchy, E. (2001). Needed: A new educational civil rights movement. *Phi Delta Kappan, 82*(7), 492–499.

Eisner, E. W. (2003). Questionable assumptions about schooling. *Phi Delta Kappan, 84*(9), 648–658.

Kaplan, L., & Owings, W. A. (2003). The politics of teacher quality. *Phi Delta Kappan, 84*(9), 687–693.

Lindeman, B. (2001). Reaching out to immigrant parents. *Educational Leadership, 58*(6), 73–77.

Mathis, W. J. (2003). No child left behind: Costs and benefits. *Phi Delta Kappan, 84*(9), 679–693.

Muklopadhyay, C., & Henze, R. C. (2003). How real is race? Using anthropology to make sense of human diversity. *Phi Delta Kappan, 84*(9), 669–679.

Nieto, S. M. (2002/2003). Profoundly multicultural questions. *Educational Leadership, 60*(4), 6–10.

Poplam, W. J. (2002/2003). A nation at risk really ought to take a few. *Educational Leadership, 60*(4), 83–86.

Posner, D. (2002). Education for the 21st century. *Phi Delta Kappan, 84*(4), 316–317.

Ramirez, A. (2001). How merit pay undermines education. *Educational Leadership, 58*(5), 21–26.

Starnes, B. A. (2006). Montana's Indian education: Toward an education worthy of American ideals. *Phi Delta Kappan, 88*(3), 184–192.

Wilms, W. W. (2003). Altering the structure and culture of American schools. *Phi Delta Kappan, 84*(8), 606–615.

Web Sites Consulted

African American Registry (2005). National Association of Women's Clubs formed! Retrieved April 8, 2005, from http://www.aaregistry.com/african_american_history/1888/national.

Alcatraz is not an island: Indian activism timeline/PBS. ITVS, 2002. Retrieved October 25, 2006, from http://www.pbs.org/itvs/alcatrazisnotanisland/timeline.html.

Asian American timeline. Pearson. Retrieved October 25, 2006, from http://www.cis.umassd.edu/~gleung/nacaf/Timeline.htm.

Civil rights movement timeline. Pearson Education. Retrieved October 25, 2006, from http://www.infoplease.com/spot/civilrightstimeline1.html.

Johnson, D. Asian-American history timeline. University of Massachusetts, 2004. Retrieved November 1, 2006, from http://www.infoplease.com/spot/asiantimeline4html.

National Association of Colored Women's Clubs. (2005). History of the National Association of Colored Women's Clubs, Inc. Retrieved April 8, 2005, from http://www.nacwc.org/about/history.php.

The Supreme Court and equal rights. Pearson Education, 2006. Retrieved October 25, 2006, from http://www.infoplease.com/timelines/equalrights.html.

Timeline of the 20th century Indian activism and federal efforts to enact self-determination, 1944 to the present. National Congress of American Indians, 2001. Retrieved October 27, 2006, from http:www.humboldt.edu/~go1/kellogg/pdf/part3h.

The voices of civil rights: The voices. AARP, 2004. Retrieved November 1, 2006, from http://www.voicesofcivilrights.org/ timeline_alt.html.

Williams, L. E. (1976). Bicentennial memories of Negroes. Retrieved May 27, 2005, from http://www.lcl.lib.mo.us.

Williams, L. S. (1995). Records of the National Association of Colored Women's Clubs, 1895–1992. Retrieved April 8, 2005, from http://www.lexisnexis.com/academic/guides/African.

http://guweb2.gonzaga.edu/faculty/campbell/enl310/winthrop.htm

http://www.nd.edu/~rbarger/www7/pur17.jp

http://www.nd.edu/~rbarger/www7/pur19.jpg

http://www.monticello.org/jefferson/biography.html

http://www.greatsite.com/timeline-english-bible-history/noah-webster.html

http://www.ushistory.org/franklin/

http://www.nd.edu/~rbarger/www7/common.html

http://www.library.wisc.edu/etext/WIReader/contents/pioneer.html

http://www.africanamericans.com/biographies.htm

http://www.historicaldocuments.com/indianremovalact.htm

http://bushong.net/dawn/about/college/ids100/workers.shtml

http://www.theodora.com/flags/mexico_flags.html

http://www.nd.edu/~rbarger/www7/common.html

http://history.evansville.net/industry.html#textile%20Industry

http://www.pbs.org/wgbh/pages/frontline/shows/race/etc/road.html

http://www.pbs.org/wgbh/pages/frontline/shows/race/etc/road.html

http://www.geocities.com/flapper_culture/

http://newdeal.feri.org/library/photo_details.cfm?PhotoID=6067&ProjCat ID =10308&CatID=15&subCatID=1063

http://www.geocities.com/flapper_culture/

http://www.coldwar.org/articles/60s/links/php3

http://www.coldwar.org/articles/50s/sputnik.php3

http://www.africanamericans.com/MLKjrNobelPeacePrize.htm

http://www.coldwar.org/articles/60s/index.php3

http://www.hq.nasa.gov/office/pao/History/sputnik/sputnik1.jpg

http://www.metcalf.ilstu.edu/curric/eighth/8decade/sixties/60smain/politics60/crmakao.htm

http://www.lucidcafe.com/library/95august/lbj.html

http://www.metcalf.ilstu.edu/curric/eighth/8decade/sixties/60smain/politics60/war_on_poverty.htm

http://www.jimmycarterlibrary.org/documents/jec/jecbio_p.phtml

http://www.whitehouse.gov/history/presidents/bc42.html

http://www.gettysburg.edu/~tshannon/his341/nep05pg2.htm

http://www.nd.edu/~rbarger/www7/common.html